WISDOM
CALLING

To Brooke—
Ps. 90:12

John

"I have never experienced a devotional like Wisdom Calling. The term 'devotional' makes me think of a merely feel-good and sometimes shallow message. Bobo's writing is NOT that. He has depth! **It is almost like I can visualize him talking to a young professional over a coffee as he unpacks Gospel truth.** All the while, I never felt like I needed an advanced seminary degree to follow along. I look forward to recommending *Wisdom Calling* to my friends!

— *Patrick; Realtor®; Charleston, SC*

"Wisdom Calling **meets the reader in a space that any Christian professional needs to confront** — how they will address their workplace/money/vocation through the lens of God's Word. An important distinction from other Christian works on these topics; is that *Wisdom Calling* does not address God's Word through the lens of the workplace but vice versa. It is a series that will be of great benefit to Christ followers everywhere."

— *David; Financial Advisor; Lancaster, PA*

WISDOM
CALLING

A PROFESSIONAL'S DEVOTIONAL GUIDE
TO SKILLFUL LIFE AND WORK

BOBO BECK

Copyright © 2022 by Bobo Beck.
All rights reserved.
Published in the United States by Wisdom Calling, an imprint of Ninety Twelve Group LLC.
Printed in the United States of America
Wisdomcalling.org
First Edition
Book design by Michelle Getz, michelle@getzcreative.com

ISBN: 979-8-9870060-0-9 (paperback)
ISBN: 979-8-9870060-1-6 (ebook)

WISDOM CALLING

DEDICATION

To my father, Ed Beck,

and my late mother, Joan Beck

Thank you for placing me on the path of wisdom

from my childhood.

CONTENTS

INTRODUCTION

"I don't know what to do, but I sure want to get this right."

"How can I learn to discern wisdom and have confidence in my decisions?"

"What exactly is wisdom, anyway?"

In my academic and career journey, I've asked these questions—and as I meet with businesspeople and nonprofit executives every week, I'm very aware of what we all struggle with as leaders.

Sure, I've been a "wise guy" much of my life but, deep down, always wanted to be someone who operated with wisdom. I bet you do, too. The good news is that it's possible. The better news is that the source of wisdom isn't Bobo Beck.

This book— and subsequent volumes, along with courses and consulting—is what I wish I could have read years ago. I hope it helps you enjoy seeing life and work from God's perspective. We need it more than ever.

THE NEED FOR MARKET-PLACE WISDOM

It is more vital than ever to know how to effectively navigate today's rapidly-changing, fast-paced world, especially for those of us engaged in business. At no other time in history has there been such a never-ending supply of information, yet such a lack of actual wisdom to know how to discern it

all. Our lives are saturated with a constant flow of noise from the news, podcasts, blogs, videos, and influencers–all vying for our attention. And as the global markets fluctuate and the daily pressures of our professional and personal lives increase, the stabilizing reality we need is actually found in an ancient, yet timeless source— the Bible.

In the Old Testament book of Proverbs, we are taught that, "the fear of the LORD is the beginning of wisdom, and the knowledge of the Holy One is insight" (9:10). Knowing and submitting to our Maker is foundational to attaining real, applicable understanding in this life.

And the whole book of Proverbs uses picturesque descriptions to fill out this experience of hearing and learning wisdom by fearing God. Throughout the book, wisdom is personified as a woman walking through the streets to plead with simple ones, scoffers, and fools to listen to and follow her words–words that ultimately will bring them life and freedom.

Wisdom cries aloud in the street, in the markets she raises her voice; at the head of the noisy streets she cries out; at the entrance of the city gates she speaks. (1:20)

This wisdom–calling out to us to listen–is essentially the skill needed to live a life that pleases God. But notice where Lady Wisdom is speaking. Her context is the marketplace, the center of community activity, filled with busyness and cacophony of life. *Are you there? Are you listening?*

My own experience in a variety of workplaces has shown me my own great need for God's wisdom in my work. I've spent time in education, real estate, consulting, ministry, and investing–gathering knowledge and experience, but all the time needing God's wisdom in every project, every sale, every deadline, every transition. The job for any one of us is to heed wisdom's call–to listen to God's Word on the topic of work.

If you are teachable and patient, you indeed will grow in your ability to not only hear and discern Lady Wisdom's voice, but also to intentionally and consistently apply biblical wisdom to your everyday life in the marketplace. Wisdom Calling is designed as a daily guide through the very words of God to provide clarity and stability for you as you conduct business, invest, manage, and make decisions.

AN OVERVIEW
I have designed this resource to provide you with daily devotional lessons that you can work through Monday to Friday over the course of 50 weeks (250 lessons total). Half of the lessons are from the Old Testament and the other half from the New Testament, providing a comprehensive, yet concise one-year study through the whole Bible on the topic of workplace wisdom. I have curated specific texts that highlight various themes and teachings that are particularly relevant to Christian professionals–such as work, rest, success, wealth, debt, and generosity, to name a

few. As you continue through the lessons, these themes will build on each other as additional insight and understanding are discussed.

I'd like to provide a short explanation of my approach in writing these Bible lessons.

CHRONOLOGICALLY ARRANGED
The first lesson begins in Genesis and will end with Revelation, following the actual timeline in which events are believed to have occurred, not necessarily the way the individual books of the Bible are arranged in our modern day translations. For example, after Deuteronomy and the life of Moses, we will jump to Psalm 90 and consider this psalm that Moses wrote. And in the New Testament, after Acts 8, we will study the book of James and then shift back to Acts since as the events in the book of Acts were unfolding, other Bible books–like James' epistle–were being written, copied, and shared around the ancient world. I've chosen this chronological approach in the hope of giving readers a fuller understanding of how various parts of the Bible are all connected.

CONTEXTUALLY AND HISTORICALLY SITUATED
The Bible, although inspired by God Himself, was written by real people to other real people in real contexts and circumstances throughout history. This is important to keep this in mind as we read and seek to understand biblical texts. Each lesson is written with consideration of the original audience and intent of the author so that we can gain the most accurate under-

standing of God's Word. Approaching Bible passages this way will help minimize any tendency to pull specific verses and phrases out of their context or try to make the Bible say what we want it to say.

EXPOSITIONALLY WRITTEN
Our approach with these lessons will be to carefully draw out the exact meaning of the passages that we are considering. At times this will include a more technical analysis from the original languages of the Bible (Hebrew and Greek) as well as occasional grammatical features. Ultimately, my desire is to offer explanations of meaning from what the Bible actually says. However, the purpose of each lesson isn't to draw out every aspect of a passage—only enough to enable our understanding of what the passage means.

CHRISTOLOGICALLY FO-CUSED
The central message of the Bible is what is called "the gospel"—the good news that God sent His Son Jesus Christ, Who lived a perfect life and died a sacrificial death so that sinners may be forgiven of their sins if they repent and believe in Him. This overarching message must remain central during this journey or else we can make the mistake of misunderstanding the purpose of the Bible as just another self-help resource to aid us in our quest to be better people.

PRACTICALLY APPLIED
I have confidence that as you study through the verses of the Bible discussed in this book, you will find God's Word to be extremely practical. What was written down thousands of years ago in specific times and places is still relevant to our own lives and work today! Not only is the Word of God still applicable today, but it is also very much needed to help us discern truth in a sea of information and noise.

SIMPLY DESIGNED
Each daily lesson includes the same elements: a short topical title; a Bible text to read; a list of keywords for the lesson; contextual, historical, and literary considerations related to the text; practical questions and suggestions for your reflection; and an example prayer to use in closing your study.

PRAYERFULLY CONSIDERED
In the New Testament book of James, the author writes, "If any of you lacks wisdom, let him ask God, who gives generously to all without reproach, and it will be given him" (1:5). I am prayerful as I compose these lessons, and my hope in writing this book is based on a belief that James' words are true: If you remain humble and allow God to teach you, He will give you the understanding and skill you need to honor him in business and to live wisely with those around you.

RETURN ON TIME INVESTMENT
As you consistently work through these 250 lessons, it is my prayer that you will experience the following results.
- Know God more intimately.
- Understand His Word more completely
- Know yourself more accurately
- Articulate your calling more clearly
- Treat others more generously
- Steward resources more effectively

SUGGESTIONS

Here are a few suggestions that will enable you to get the most out of this journey.

1 Pick a specific time each day to work through a lesson. It will take you 15-20 minutes to read the text and then work through the study. Ideally, try to do this at the start of your day before you get too busy.

2 Try to block out as many distractions as possible as you start a lesson. Turn off your phones if you are able. Position yourself in a place and posture where you can focus.

3 Take a brief moment to quiet your heart and mind in prayer, asking the Holy Spirit to guide and teach you, to give you the wisdom you need from God's Word.

4 Discipline yourself to read the entire Bible text noted at the top of each lesson. This will be the most important aspect of each lesson in many ways—so don't skip over it. As with many realities of life, you will get out of this what you intentionally put in.

5 If you're able, connect with a community of others and share openly with them what you are reflecting on and where you need to act in response to the wisdom you gain from God's Word during the study. Sharing on social media is another way to encourage friends with what you are learning.

Blessed is the one who finds wisdom, and the one who gets understanding, for the gain from her is better than gain from silver and her profit better than gold. She is more precious than jewels, and nothing you desire can compare with her. Long life is in her right hand; in her left hand are riches and honor. Her ways are ways of pleasantness, and all her paths are peace. She is a tree of life to those who lay hold of her; those who hold her fast are called blessed. Proverbs 3:13-18

May you experience the blessing of God in all its fullness as you seek after wisdom. To the praise of His glorious grace!

Bobo

THE FIRST & ULTIMATE ENTREPRENEUR

Read: Genesis 1:1-25 (3-4 minutes)

In the beginning, God created the heavens and the earth... and God *said*... God *called*... and God *made*... and God *saw*... and God *set*... So God *created*... and God *blessed*... And God *saw* that it was good.

DISCUSS + MEDITATE

Welcome to a yearlong journey together. We start with a look back to where it all began–Genesis. Penned by Moses, this book of beginnings forms the introductory section of the *Torah*–also called the Law, which includes the first five books of the Old Testament and would first have been presented to those living in modern-day Iraq.

This passage is truly "big picture": We get a macro vantage point as the Creator-God, named *Elohim,* begins His work of constructing the cosmos. This name for God indicates his strength and power as shown by His works as Creator, Sustainer, and supreme Judge of the world. And the verses in our reading for today tell us what He did: God created (The Hebrew word *bara'* means "make" or "manufacture") the skies above and the land beneath–all of which was "without form and void." Elohim created with just words ("And God said..."), and He fashioned the heavens and earth "out of nothing"--i.e., with no pre-existing materials.

Over the course of six days, God worked. He spoke light into existence and intentionally formed what he named "day" and "night,"

morning and evening, inaugurating weekly cycles as a pattern for His creation to follow. He created the five layers of our atmosphere. By gathering the waters below, He expertly crafted what he called "earth" and the "seas." God as Creator filled His creation with vegetation and trees, all within precise classification and order. He added the sun, moon, and stars to His system, each with its own function to rule and seamlessly serve the rest of His creative order. On days five and six, God filled the skies, waters, and land with creatures of every kind, including human beings. And all of this was good (the Hebrew word means "agreeable, pleasant") to Him.

The Creator-God, exceptional and all-powerful, developed this temple in which to dwell and display His glory, His magnificence, His unique greatness. And as we read these first twenty-five verses of the Bible, we realize that every microscopic molecule and every distant, unknown galaxy points to the One at the very beginning and center of it all.

REFLECT + ACT

» The Creator-God is completely self-governing and supreme over His creation, including you and me. He does not need us to exist. He intentionally created everything–simply with a word. He is God and we are not. Take a moment and reflect on whether at times you live as if God doesn't exist–in your relationships, business, or recreation.Take time to confess that you are not God, no matter how accomplished you might be at this point in your life and career.

» The Bible is about God, start to finish. Although we will be focusing on topics such as money and possessions as they emerge in the biblical text, the Bible truly isn't about us or those topics. The Christian faith focuses on one God, unlike the original Babylonian, Mesopotamian, and Egyptian religions that believed in and worshiped many gods of their own imaginations. As modern-day Christians, in a culture that increasingly mixes various religions and worldviews, resolve in your heart to know and follow *only* One, the true and living Creator-God, Elohim.

» This chapter calls us to simply sit in awe, celebrating the fact that God marvelously made all of this natural world we live in. Consider taking a 30-minute break to get outside, be in nature, and thank God for His creation.

» God's good, creative design of this world serves as the framework for the order and structure that you and I can bring to our respective businesses and organizations. God is in a sense the first and ultimate entrepreneur. By serving and acknowledging Him alone as Creator-God in all areas of your life, you root the mission and vision for your daily work in

Him. One of the most tangible ways to gauge whether you are doing this is by tracking how often you are pausing to pray to Him. You can acknowledge His presence as you commute or get set up in your home office. You can ask for His will to be done in and through you during the day or before an important meeting. You can pause to thank Him for his leadership and provision. Growing in prayer might be one of the most important disciplines you can develop during the course of this Bible study.

PRAYER

Self-existent, all-powerful Creator-God, I humbly come to You in prayer at the start of this new devotional journey. I want more than anything else to know You more and more each day. I want to understand Your Word more clearly and then have a greater resolve to follow it, modeling my work after Your creative and orderly work. You alone are God. I confess that at times I don't live my life with this reality in mind. All of the marketing and influencers of this world strategically and consistently remind me that I am in control, that "I am the master of my fate and the captain of my soul."[1] But I acknowledge that this is not true and never will be. Grant me the wisdom today to discern those kinds of godless voices and grant me the strength to look to You alone. Amen.

[1] "Invictus," William Ernest Henley

CREATED TO CREATE

Read: Genesis 1:26-31 (1-2 minutes)
So God created man in his own image… And God blessed them. And God said to them, "Be fruitful and multiply and fill the earth and subdue it and have dominion…"

DISCUSS + MEDITATE

On the sixth and final day of creation, God filled the land with living creatures–from livestock and small crawlers to large game. He then crowned creation with His greatest handiwork–human life. The divine Plurality ("Let *us* make… after *our*…") chose to fashion mankind in a way that resembled God–*in his own image* (the Hebrew word means replica or likeness). You and I and every human being that has ever existed, whether born or unborn, possess the *imago Dei* (Latin for "image of God"). Though not fully unpacked in this passage, God's sovereignly stamped image on each and every person carries with it the unique ability to reason and distinguish morality in a way the plants and animals cannot.

God created two distinct types of human beings: male and female. God ordained the distinction of gender and subsequently the institution of marriage. This unique relationship between the man and woman would establish the family as the basic building block for every society and civilization.

God gave these first humans, and all who would follow, a mandate–"let them have dominion"--authorizing them to represent His rule with a form of co-rule or a rule underneath God's ultimate reign over all. This is the language of royalty. In Elohim's creation there are no persons or classes of humans that are lesser than others; all have royal blood running through their veins. We are all, though diverse, unified via the same kinship. And we are further called to fill the earth with more and more image-bearers: He says, "Be fruitful and multiply and fill the earth." Ultimately, this is a directive for men and women to marry, have children, raise families, and live in community with others.

As image bearers, humans are also to exercise stewardship over the rest of God's creation ("have dominion," "subdue"). The idea here is that you and I are to make the earth's resources beneficial for ourselves and our families as well as for the common good of broader humanity. This is a call, from the very beginning of life on this planet, to utilize knowledge and skills necessary for wise scientific investigation and technological development. We are to steward the earth and govern it with responsibility, not exploiting it to satisfy human greed.

17

REFLECT + ACT

» All life has intrinsic value and worth, from the baby inside the mother's womb, to the geopolitical refugee, to the child with Down's Syndrome, to the night custodian at your office, to the grandmother with dementia in an assisted living facility. How does your specific work reinforce this truth of the value of human life? How might your work undermine it?

» Every human being possesses the image of the Creator-God and has a common kinship. There is no place, especially for Christians, to look down upon or treat anyone as less of a person or as part of some lower class. Though still rampant in the various industries and institutions in our world, and often just under the surface, there is no place for classism, racism, sexism, or ableism (discrimnation against people with disabilities). Reflect on whether you can identify traces of these discriminatory attitudes in your own heart or mind first and then have the courage to speak out as you see them manifested around you.

» What are some specific skills that you would still like to develop? Consider writing them down and taking the steps needed to acquire them. Share your desires with a trusted friend or ally. What motivates you to continue to grow and learn, whether personally or professionally? Is it simply ambition? Is it greed? Do you find yourself motivated to outperform others? Or do you have a broader goal to see God use you for His glory and for the common good of your sphere of influence and community?

» Do you try to practice environmental stewardship and conservation? Do you take care of this earth—not as a self-righteous means of showing how great you are or by superficially participating in a good cause, but as a conscientious steward of God's creation? Find ways to preserve the earth's resources so that they can be a continual source of benefit for yourself and those around you.

» Read the lyrics of and/or listen to the hymn, "I Sing the Mighty Power of God" by Isaac Watts (published1715)[2].

PRAYER

Gracious Creator, You indeed are a kind and generous Provider. You have lavished us with Your amazing and beautiful creation. Every sunrise and sunset proclaim Your wonder. The night sky tells of Your fathomless mystery. The oceans speak to the depth of Your wisdom. "While all that borrows life from Thee is ever in Thy care; And everywhere that we can be, Thou, God, art present there."[3] What a promise this is! And what a reality that You have created me in Your image and have crowned me to help rule over Your earthly domain. It is indeed true that "there is not a square inch in the whole domain of our human existence over which Christ, who is Sovereign over all, does not cry, Mine!"[4] Help me bask in this truth today as I seek the common good of those within my sphere. Amen.

[2] Public Domain.
[3] "I Sing the Mighty Power of God," stanza 3.
[4] Abraham Kuyper, inaugural address, dedication of the Free University

AS GARDENERS & GUARDIANS

Read: Genesis 2:1-15 (2 mins.)

God finished his work that he had done... and there was no man to work the ground... The LORD God took the man and put him in the garden of Eden to work it and keep it.

DISCUSS + MEDITATE

As we have clearly seen, Elohim was very active in the process of ordering creation. Notice once again the language from these first two chapters: God created (1:1), God separated (1:4), God made (1:7; 1:16), God set (1:17), God *finished his work* (2:2), LORD God *formed* the man (2:7), LORD God *planted* a garden (2:8), and the rib... from the man...he *made* into a woman (2:22). The Creator was on a trade mission from the beginning. His initial work was to arrange the heavens and the earth as His temple, a divine sanctuary. And it was all good.

Work necessitates work.The passage states that there was no human being to "work the ground" and "keep it" (Gen. 2:5, 15). The Hebrew word for work (abad) carries the idea of serving and toiling. There's a direct connection in this context with the actual ground itself and the need to irrigate and till it so that it was more conducive for plant growth. To "keep" (the Hebrew word samar) was a managerial function–the first humans were to preserve, watch over, and guard all that was in the garden.

From the very beginning, before sin entered the picture, God developed productive work as part of His good purpose for mankind. We learn from this that working and keeping the creation is part of the very essence of being human. So here in the garden, God gave man a purposeful existence–a God-given assignment, not a cursed condition.

REFLECT + ACT

» The reality that work in and of itself is not a curse is pretty countercultural today. It's commonplace to gripe and complain about having to go to work. Our jobs, though necessary for income, seem only to get in the way of our weekends and vacations. What is your current attitude regarding work in general? How does your job or career in particular play into this mindset?

» God has called each one of us to oversee and manage the environment He created. This certainly includes actual environmental preservation and conservation. But more importantly, our care of the environment means we are to use the resources around us–or find ways to acquire ones that are needed–to serve the common good of others. We are to bring order where there is chaos, calm where there is noise, and healing where there is brokenness. Think about your professional work or ministries you are a part of. In what ways are you bringing order, structure, and healing? Or, in what ways can you start to bring about these various fruits of productive work in God's world?

» Being productive, as we have been reminded, was God's plan for humanity from the beginning. And we can often find our primary identity actually in the work that we spend the most time and energy on. This is natural in many ways: when meeting someone for the first time, it's common to ask what kind of work someone does. But think about those who have a disabling physical or mental condition. Think about those who are retired, the elderly who are not as productive as they used to be, or even those who are unemployed. Think about the lack of purpose and meaning they might struggle with. Perhaps you yourself are underemployed or working a job that clearly does not maximize your gifts and calling. Whether your own situation is challenging or you are concerned for the vocational limitations of others, submit these circumstances to the Lord and ask Him to provide wisdom. He is more than capable of doing so.

PRAYER

LORD God, it is indeed You Who designed work from the beginning. You demonstrated Your genius through ordering creation. You then set man in the garden to work and keep it as stewards, as faithful managers. Though sin messed everything up, we are still called to be wise stewards today. I am not an owner. My money is not mine. My car is not mine. My house or apartment are not mine, whether my name is on the paperwork or not. I am simply a manager of the things You have entrusted to me, including my work. Thank you for giving me the ability to work, to have the mental and physical strength to do what I do each day. I want to work in a way that makes Your greatness visible and benefits those around me. I pray now on behalf of those that I know who are not able to work or are currently looking for work. Would you encourage and provide for them? May all of us find our purpose and meaning in You. In Jesus' name, amen.

REST, HURRY & HUSTLE

Read: Genesis 2:1-3

Thus the heavens and the earth were finished, and all the host of them. And on the seventh day God finished his work that he had done, and he *rested* on the seventh day from all the work that he had done. So God blessed the seventh day and made it holy, because on it God rested from all his work that he had done in creation.

DISCUSS + MEDITATE

After six days, God's work of creating was finished. He had completed the process of ordering creation, and He rested (from the Hebrew word šābat, the root of sabbath). This wasn't a rest because God was tired or weary–quite the contrary. In this context rest indicated effortless ease and a sense of completion and achievement. With the earth as His divine sanctuary, there were still certain activities included as part of His resting: *finishing, blessing, making holy.* By consecrating the seventh day in this way, God intentionally took this day from common use, sanctified it, and set it apart to be devoted to him.

But this was not to be a day for just Him alone. Rather, in blessing and setting this day of rest apart, the Creator-God provided this day as a gift to be shared with the rest of the world. What a wise and gracious Creator! In His infinite wisdom, He knew from the beginning that His image-bearers would not have the sustainable ability to labor and toil days on end with no break or rest. Human beings were providentially designed with limitations. And this is good.

Taking one day out of every seven to cease from normal, common routines is a divinely inspired way of reorienting our mental perspectives and physical bodies. This day of rest wasn't specified as a full day of sleep or complete inactivity, but rather a different kind of activity. God intended this day for worship and celebration, somewhat like a declaration of freedom from work for a day. It's a day where humans pause from their work in order to meet with God their Creator, reconnect with Him at the deepest level of their beings, and declare that their work does not ultimately control or define who they are.

REFLECT + ACT

》 How does this God-ordained understanding of purposeful rest impact you? Do today's passage and discussion come as a relief to you or do they trigger annoyance that God intentionally restrains our work and productivity? Overworking violates God's design for human nature, regardless of what the productivity experts and achiever-oriented influencers say. How would you describe your current work-rest rhythm? Take time to think about this and be willing to make some changes–perhaps even radical ones.

» We will discuss the actual Jewish Sabbath and its New Testament applications in later devotional lessons. But for now, the key is to see that God ordained and gifted one full 24-hour period weekly for His glory, for our rest and joy, and for the good of those around us. This break is increasingly countercultural, especially in Western societies. We live and work in a world that values speed, hustle, activity, and productivity. And a first step in applying the wisdom of God's weekly break plan, inaugurated in Genesis, is to be aware of this modern cultural phenomenon of busyness and how it impacts you each day.

» Many of us work during the daytime from Monday through Friday, approximately 40 hours a week. This leaves Saturday or Sunday as a time to rest in the full sense of that term as we have discussed. In Jewish culture, a day would actually start at sundown. So, using that definition of a "day," a Sabbath could start on a Friday night at sundown and extend until Saturday night at sundown, or it could go from Saturday night to Sunday night. Most Christians today choose to set aside Sundays for this purpose since that is also the day many of us worship with our local church communities.

» The point here is not which day, but that we set aside a day out of our week to worship God, celebrate all of His marvelous works, and declare our freedom that we are not enslaved to our overworked culture–we can rest.

» Some Christians don't observe a day of rest because they think they can't afford to take a day off, that work still needs to be done, or that less economic production will be detrimental to their goals or to the expectations others have of them. But this mentality couldn't be further from the truth. Deeply rested people are the most productive. For an interesting case study, read the history of Chick-fil-A, one of the largest American fast food restaurant chains. S. Truett Cathy, a devoted Christian, founded the restaurant in 1946 just outside of Atlanta, Georgia, and chose from the beginning to close on Sundays, despite the dire warnings from financial experts at the time.[5]

» For more on this topic, read *To Hell with the Hustle* (Bethke, 2019)[6] and *The Ruthless Elimination of Hurry* (Comer, 2019)[7]

PRAYER
Heavenly Father, thank You for the gift of rest. Thank you for this reminder that I have limitations–I am not You. Help me continue to discern the pull towards and glorification of hurry and activity and productivity in today's culture. And help me by Your grace to live my life from the Sabbath, to find my daily and weekly rest in You alone. I want to be productive in my work, but I want to do so from a place of purposeful rest and worship. Help me even this week to use one full day to worship and celebrate You. In Jesus' name, amen.

[5]https://www.entrepreneur.com/article/311452.
[6]https://jeffandalyssa.com/books/.
[7]https://johnmarkcomer.com.

PARADISE LOST

Read: Genesis 3:1-24 (3 minutes)
Cursed is the ground because of you; *in pain* you shall eat of it all the days of your life; *thorns* and *thistles* it shall bring forth for you...By the *sweat* of your face you shall eat bread.

DISCUSS + MEDITATE

After reading today's passage, you probably feel the weight of the reality of what took place when Adam and Eve first sinned: A man and woman in a perfect environment in perfect communion with the Creator, in such an unexplainable fashion, disregarded God's instructions and willfully rebelled against him. Did you see the subtlety of the serpent–how he presented a half-truth, telling Eve that she and Adam would not indeed "surely die" as God had said? (Gen. 3:1) Did you see how they believed the lie that God's Word was subject to their own interpretation? Did you read how they ultimately and utterly failed in their assignment to guard all that was in the garden, including each other? At the root of their sinful decisions were unbelieving minds and discontented hearts. They literally were allowed to fully partake of everything God had created for them, but they still desired more–so much so that they were willing to test God and risk death.

The serpent tempted them with the ability to reinvent their lives and achieve an even higher and deeper enlightened state ("You will be like God"). Yes it sounded pleasant and delightful. But it was all a fantasy. The intoxicating promise of unbridled success, mental enrichment, and self-fulfillment–he said it would "make one wise"--was too much to pass up. And in the end, that serpent-promise failed to deliver. The arrogant false system erected for the first humans to outwit the Creator-God immediately began to crumble.

With the sin of our original parents, the entire cosmos was thrown into chaos and disorder. It would never be the same. There would now be hardship and frustration in their daily efforts to work the land and subdue it. There would be pain and suffering. There would no longer be abundant productivity. Never again would image-bearers fully be able to subdue the earth. And this curse would extend to the whole of creation and exists in our modern times.

Yet remarkably, in the midst of this doom and death, there was a glimmer of light. In God's judgment pronounced to the serpent, God foreshadowed a time when one of Adam's descendants ("offspring") would be bruised, but ultimately would crush and defeat the serpent and all of his dominion. Adam then gave his wife the name Eve, which meant "life," another glimmer of hope. And as we look back at this scene from our vantage point, we know this offspring of Adam to be none other than Jesus Christ. As we continue this journey through the Scriptures, we will see this promise fulfilled.

REFLECT + ACT

» The ramifications of Adam and Eve's sin and the subsequent curse are many and there are multiple reflections to consider. I would encourage you to spend the necessary time processing all of them. Allow the weight of this cataclysmic event to impact you. Take some time to properly grieve: We are still under the original curse and are touched by it every day in various ways. Entire global movements, economies, governments, international partnerships, Fortune 500 corporations, and even our own companies and organizations–all are impacted by sin. Yet the Bible looks to a time when nature and our world will be set free from the consequences of human sin. Hold both of these realities in tension as you work today–we live in a world of sin, and we have hope for a future world without it.

» Think about the draw of self-fulfillment and enlightenment. This is not just a Genesis 3 experience–it is still prevalent today as it was at the beginning of civilization. Almost every marketing campaign and advertisement promises to provide a product or service that can help us achieve success, reach a heightened level of sophistication, obtain the good life, etc. It's endless. And most of these ads tap into the innate greed and discontent within our hearts and minds. "Maybe I can actually be like God if x happens," we are tempted to think. This kind of godless thinking is also at the core of many of the tech gurus of our day, intent on creating alternative realities or environments like the metaverse where humans create their own existence.

» Be careful when listening to so many of the influencers, gurus, and experts of our day. They often offer many half-truths and can lure you with the same under-delivering promise of enlightenment that tempted Adam and Eve. Who are you listening to right now? Podcasts? Social media voices? Authors? Reflect on how the information you regularly and how these sources are influencing you regarding self.

PRAYER

Creator-God, this passage from Genesis is very weighty. Thank You for preserving Your Word and for giving me the time to read it and process its impact in my life and work. Thank You for reminding me of the universal and awful curse of sin along with the knowledge that one day the curse will be lifted in Christ. Until then, would You give me the discernment I need to understand the longings and desires of my own heart, the areas where I am not content in You? Would you give me added discernment as I listen to the voices around me? Protect me from believing subtle lies. You alone are God and I am not. Help me live in this reality today by Your grace. In Jesus' name, amen.

WORK AS WORSHIP

6

Read: Genesis 4:1-16 (2 minutes)
Now Abel was a keeper of sheep, and Cain a *worker* of the ground. . . And the Lord had regard for Abel and his *offering,* but for Cain and his offering he had no regard. So Cain was very angry, and his face fell.
* Also read or skim through Genesis 4:17-26

DISCUSS + MEDITATE

In this passage we see the beginning of civilized life, the literal carrying out of the "be fruitful and multiply" mandate, and the gruesome reality of life under the curse of sin. The narrative of Cain and Abel adds to our understanding of the nature of work as designed by God. Work in this passage is interwoven with worship of Yahweh ("the LORD"), the personal name of God that highlights His covenant relationship with His people. Although Abel's animal husbandry work and Cain's agricultural work were different, God had room to accept them both as worship. However, there was something in Cain's heart and life–not fully revealed in the text–that nullified his offering to the LORD. His work-worship wasn't authentic or spiritual. Filled with jealousy and rage, he then plotted and killed his own brother, another image-bearer of God.

The curse of sin is then intensified for Cain–he would no longer be as fruitful and productive as he once was (4:12). He would be exiled from his home region, condemned to wander as a fugitive (4:14). What followed was Cain's attempt at independence and self-sufficiency from God. In many ways he and his family were successful: His son built a city (4:17), his descendants made tents (4:20) and musical instruments (4:21), and some developed skill in metal-working (4:22). They lived semi-nomadic lifestyles, and their focus on arts and crafts.

Yet, sin was always "crouching at the door" (4:7). Cain and his family, in a sense, became a microcosm of technical prowess, but also moral failure. There was potential for good and blessing, but also evil and abuse. Their skill with metal led to the making of weapons designed for death and destruction. Lamech, seven generations from Cain, took two wives (4:19) and bragged about killing a young boy for a simple slight (4:23-24).

The darkness was briefly lifted as God blessed Adam and Eve with another child, Seth–a "replacement" for Abel (4:25). The text says, "At that time people began to call upon the name of the LORD" (4:26). There was still hope. God was still at work to preserve a descendant Who would one day crush the head of the serpent (3:15).

REFLECT + ACT

» Have you ever viewed your career and the work that you do as worship? Most of us spend 40+ hours a week engaged in our professions and only one to two hours a week in actual corporate worship. So, overwhelmingly we have more opportunity to serve and please God through our daily work than we do through our weekly church event attendance. Here are some tangible ways to begin integrating your work into worship:

Talk to God through prayer as you are commuting or preparing to begin your work each day. Express gratitude for your job and for the ability to perform your responsibilities.

Pray to God for your colleagues, employees (if you are in a position of leadership), leaders, and clients/customers. Ask God to bless them and work in their lives.

When you're tired or stressed or frustrated, try to step away for a few minutes to pray, read the Bible, or listen to an encouraging song. Focus on God and Who He is instead of your work for a moment.

Be quick to give God the credit for your progress, productivity, and accomplishments, both in the day-to-day wins and on the stage during awards season.

» Being successful in business is not always a direct sign of God's presence and blessing. It can sometimes be the result of God leaving you to your own devices. Cain and his descendants were "successful," but were completely cut off from the LORD. Take a moment to think about the constant pull of society toward self-sufficiency– the idea that you can pull yourself up by your own boot straps and make anything happen, the temptation to be "self-made." If needed, take the time to ask God for forgiveness and resolve not to think in these ways.

PRAYER

Heavenly Father, I come to You now, reminded from Genesis 4 that life apart from You is futile. My work is not an end in itself but rather a daily means of worshiping You. You are the great provider. You are the One Who has given me the physical and intellectual abilities to be productive and flourish. Forgive me for not acknowledging this as frequently as I should and for allowing the world around me to influence how I think about myself and my work. I want to grow in seeing my work as worship, and I want to be more effective at recognizing society's pull towards independence and self-sufficient success. I can't do this on my own. May my life through my work be a tangible testimony of Your active presence and blessing, giving me joy in You, benefiting those around me, and bringing You glory. Amen.

WORK AS RENEWAL

Read: Genesis 6:1-13; 7:23-24; 8:20-22; 9:1 (2-3 minutes)
Out of the ground that the Lord has *cursed*, this one shall bring us *relief* from our *work* and from the *painful toil* of our hands.

DISCUSS + MEDITATE

This lesson covers a much wider swath of biblical text, spanning 1600 years from Adam to Noah. Generations went by (5:1-28) until the Bible records the words of a father, Lamech: "Out of the ground that the Lord has cursed, this one shall bring us relief from our work and from the painful toil of our hands" (5:29). "This one" was Lamech's newborn son Noah, whose name meant "rest" or "relief" and who grew to be righteous, blameless, walking with God (6:9). Noah and his family were the exception in a society that was increasingly wicked, corrupt, and violent (6:11,13). God had had enough. The text states that God was grieved– He regretted creating mankind and planned to judge humanity for sin. After making a covenant with Noah (6:18), God did, in fact, judge all the inhabitants of the earth at that time by means of a forty-day flood. All of His creation–that He had once pronounced "good"--were then completely destroyed (chapter 7).

"But God remembered Noah" (8:1) and his family and all the animals Noah had stowed away in the ark. When the flood waters finally subsided, this faithful remnant of people began again the quest to "be fruitful and multiply" and have dominion over the earth (8:17; 9:1,7). The imago Dei lived on as the covenant-keeping God made a way, offering renewal to the earth that He had created and destroyed. And what was the first thing Noah and his family did after months of being cooped up during the flood? They worshiped Yahweh (8:20). They offered a sacrifice to the LORD, showing gratitude for His deliverance and consecrating the new earth that they would soon begin to subdue and cultivate.

The text then states that the LORD promised to never destroy the earth in that way ever again (8:21). This did not mean that there would never be localized flooding or other natural disasters–just nothing destructive on a global scale. The LORD then reestablished the natural rhythms of seasons ("summer and winter"), climates ("cold and heat"), time periods ("day and night"), and agriculture ("seedtime and harvest"). These rhythms have been around for thousands of years and form the context in which we work, rest, and reap today.

REFLECT + ACT

» I want to be careful in trying to draw

a direct parallel between the times of Noah and our society today. But it is safe to say that as our civilization continues to grow, wickedness and corruption and violence are growing as well. We have the opportunity to stand out as part of a faithful remnant today, to take God at His word, and to simply obey what He has commanded us to do. Several times in the text we studied today, God states that Noah "did all that the LORD had commanded" (6:22; 7:5; 7:16). Resolve in your heart right now to obey God. Seek His power and courage in order to do so, regardless of the cost. If needed, take a moment to repent of any specific areas of your life where you are clearly disobeying him.

» God is in control of creation and purposely reestablished the rhythms of nature after the flood. Be encouraged as you listen to or read the words of the hymn "Great is Thy Faithfulness"[8]:

(verse two)
Summer and winter, and springtime and harvest
Sun, moon, and stars in their courses above.
Join with all nature in manifold witness
To Thy great faithfulness, mercy and love.

(chorus)
Great is Thy faithfulness! Great is Thy faithfulness!
Morning by morning new mercies I see.
All I have needed Thy hand hath provided.
Great is Thy faithfulness, Lord, unto me!

PRAYER

God thank You for Your Word. Thank You for Your intentional work in saving Noah and his family as a testament to Your mercy and faithfulness to Your covenant. Indeed, great is your faithfulness, throughout all of time and in my own life. I am reminded that, as in the days of Noah, I live in a world that is wicked and corrupt and increasing in violence. Help me not to become numb to this reality or succumb to its addicting influence. I want to obey You and be faithful to You in my generation. But I need Your power. I need to have courage that is not natural to me. Thank You for this reminder that You are worthy to be trusted. You do what You say You will do. Help me to be trustworthy and faithful in my sphere of influence and in my networks. I want to join with all nature in witness to Your faithfulness, mercy, and love. Grant me the grace to do so. Amen.

[8]Thomas Chisholm (1923).

BABEL INC.

Read: Genesis 10:8-11 and Genesis 11:1-9 (2-3 minutes)
Then they said, "Come, let us build ourselves a city and a tower with its top in the heavens, and let us make a name for ourselves, lest we be dispersed over the face of the whole earth."

DISCUSS + MEDITATE

The new civilization began to spread through the family of Noah into what is now Africa, Asia, Europe, and the Mediterranean region. They were obeying God's renewed command to be fruitful and multiply (9:7). Three generations later we are introduced to Noah's great-grandson, Nimrod, "the first on earth to be a mighty man...a mighty hunter" (10:8, 9). These descriptions highlight the fact that he had become a warrior and champion by dominating the surrounding clans and lands. Nimrod utilized personal prowess and political power, a philosophy counter to the creation mandate and antithetical to humans being vice-regents of God on earth. And two of the kingdoms he established–Babel & Nineveh– would later become the headquarters of the Babylonian and Assyrian empires, direct enemies of the people of God.

The text states that Nimrod and the people with him migrated, deciding to settle in one location and develop a city together. No longer would they live their semi-nomadic lifestyle and continue to "fill the earth". Now they became sedentary and began unifying themselves, using their skills and resources collectively. Their efforts to build a city were more a quest to determine and establish their own destiny without the LORD. They harvested bitumen from the ground (a petroleum-based substance) and advanced brickmaking in an effort to construct a tower that would help them make a name for themselves and would provide security against dispersion (11:4). By coming together in this way, they tried not only to preserve their identity but also to control their fortunes. However, their enterprise was short-lived. God intervened by intentionally mixing their language abilities, thus making it nearly impossible for them to continue to be unified (11:8-9).

REFLECT + ACT

≫ Think about Nimrod once again– this man who displayed an incredible amount of personal ambition and political power. He did so at the expense of people. And his example provided a profile for so many individuals of influence to follow throughout history, even until our present day. Why is it that humans–that you and I–are so often drawn to those who have power and exercise the ability to dominate others? We see this is in the political arena at all levels of government, from local issues to the federal and international ones. But this is also frequently seen in the business world and the competitive nature of so many of our industries and companies. Market share. Monopolies. Mergers and acquisitions. So often they are simply rooted in ambition, power, and dominance. God's plan is for His created beings, especially His people, to be instruments that nurture, cultivate, and empower. Take some time to process this. Jot down some of your thoughts.

》 The city and tower of Babel, as well as the later development of Babylon, have come to symbolize human ambition, autonomy, independence, and self-sufficiency apart from God. Pop culture references this place: David Gray's song *Babylon* (1998),[9] alluding to an exiled relationship and Lady Gaga's (2020)[10] song by the same name includes lyrics like, "We only have the weekend, You can serve it to me, ancient city style, We can party like it's B.C., With a pretty 16th-century smile." Babel Inc. might not be a real Fortune 500 company, but it is alive and thriving and essentially embodies the culture that we live in. Technological advances. Social unity. Ambition. Confidence in our own abilities. May God give us the discernment to see this worldly, godless tendency of our culture and provide us with even more strength to resist self-sufficiency.

》 Unity and peace are not always ultimate goods. We live in a society that has elevated unity by means of tolerance and acceptance at all costs. Much of the biblical truth that we've already discussed in these lessons is viewed by many today as archaic dogma that serves only as an impediment to a unified, secular utopia. This antipathy toward God and the Bible

will undoubtedly increase in the months and years to come. Resolve in your heart and mind once again to know, believe, and follow the Word of God over secular humanism that seeks to exalt human autonomy and minimize the presence of God in every aspect of our society. This isn't a call for you to be rude or pugnacious, but rather to double down on your commitment to truth in an increasingly, relativistic culture.

PRAYER

Heavenly Father, You are abundant in mercy. Throughout history, people, organizations, and nations have conspired to use their collective power and influence to make names for themselves—to have others worship and admire them. I confess I am often drawn to human power and the ability, identity, and security it can provide. Thank You for this reminder today that You have Your ways of keeping us humble. Though I live in a culture that proactively exalts and rewards autonomy and ambition, help me to find my sufficiency in and through You alone. Help me to work hard, to be productive and fruitful in my vocation. And help me to be ambitious to support and encourage those around me, in ways that will increase eternal investments. I need Your grace once again. Amen.

[9]David Gray, Babylon, White Ladder, 1998.
[10]Lady Gaga, Babylon, Concord Music Publishing LLC, 2020.

GOING WITHOUT KNOWING

Read: Genesis 12:1-20 (3-4 minutes)
And I will make of you a great nation, and I will bless you and make your name great, so that you will be a blessing

DISCUSS + MEDITATE

The historical narrative now shifts from a general survey of history to the specific family of Noah's son Shem, a family that would later generate the chosen people of God, Israel. There were ten generations from Adam to Noah, and now ten more from Noah to Abram. The text states that Abram's father took his family from Ur, a highly cultured urban context located in Babylonia, the region Nimrod initially developed (11:31). From Ur (modern-day Iraq), Terah led his family to settle in Haran (modern-day Turkey). And itt was in Haran that Terah died, leaving Abram the full responsibility for the family and all their possessions. It was also in Haran that the LORD (Yahweh) singled Abram out to start another journey—a long trip south to the land of Canaan, but also a broader mission to establish a new people group and nation.

Yahweh called Abram to believe in Him and His promise, to be willing to give up his personal identity and security in order to be a conduit of blessing to a new people and the international community this people would interact with. With all human support largely removed, Abram had to forsake all and follow God, exchanging the known for the unknown.

In this passage, we see Abram catch the vision the LORD had given him and respond in faith to God's promises by obeying him. *Heard. Saw. Believed. Obeyed.* Abram led his family to the land of Canaan. And when after some time that region was devastated by severe famine, Abram led his family South to Egypt where there was water and fertile ground (12:10-20). The vision of God's blessing was still in place, but it would soon be put to a significant test. When calculating the potential threat involving his wife and Egypt's Pharaoh, Abram trusted in his own intuition, compromised his moral integrity with deception, and allowed fear to take control—all apart from the LORD.

In the end, it took a series of God-ordained plagues to remedy the situation and to get Abram's family safely out of Egypt and back to the land the LORD had promised. God intervened once again and demonstrated His faithfulness, even against the backdrop of Abram's compromise.

REFLECT + ACT

>> Leadership author and pastor Andy Stanley defines *vision* as "a clear mental picture of what could be, fueled by the

conviction that it should be."[11] In this passage, the LORD gives Abram a clear mental picture of what was possible in and through his life and in turn, Abram responded with conviction, courage, and faith. What is God's vision for your life? You are certainly not called to become the "father of many nations," but you are called to something. What is that for you? Have you heard, seen, believed, and obeyed God? What is it that He has placed deep within you that He wants to give birth to and cultivate and use to be a blessing to others? Maybe in the past you had clear leading from God to obey in some area of your life but you never obeyed. I encourage you to allow God this week to provide you with a clear mental picture of what He wants for your life and then provide the conviction to begin acting upon it.

» Take a moment to reflect on Abram's compromise and deception. Ultimately, he relied on his own calculation and intuition without consulting with the LORD, and it nearly cost him his life and everything he owned. How do you typically make decisions, especially ones that will affect others? Do you routinely commit decisions to the Lord in prayer? Do you seek out input from godly advisors within your sphere of influence? Potential compromise and deception can be avoided in our lives if we allow God to speak into our decisions on a regular basis. Ask God to forgive you if you have acted with deception or tried to forge your own way without Him. Seek restitution with others if needed. Turn from your self-sufficient decision-making and trust in the Lord to lead and bless in your life and work.

» *Read Visioneering* (2005)[12] by Andy Stanley as well as *Dream Big* (2020)[13] by Bob Goff.

PRAYER
Faithful Father, thank You once again for Your Word. Thank You for preserving it so that I can read it and know You all of these years later. As I think about Your ordained plan for my life, I ask You to provide me with clarity on how and where You want me to invest my time, energy, resources, and skills. I don't aim to make my name great. So, I need knowledge of Your will and conviction and courage to respond in faith, taking steps to see Your vision for me become a reality. My faith can quickly turn to fear like Abram's, and I can be susceptible to deception and compromise as well. Would You help me today as I navigate the temptations around me and as I seek to serve You? I ask You to bless me and to use me to be a blessing to others. In Jesus' name. Amen.

[11]Andy Stanley, Visioneering, Multnomah, 2005, p. 18.
[12]https://andystanley.com/resources/.
[13]https://www.bobgoff.com/read.

STEWARDING THE BLESSING

Read: Genesis 13:1-18 (3-4 minutes)

The land could not support both of them dwelling together; for their possessions were so great that they could not dwell together, and there was strife between the herdsmen of Abram's livestock and the herdsmen of Lot's livestock.

DISCUSS + MEDITATE

Just as soon as Abram and his family left Egypt, they encountered some major challenges. One main issue arose from within– the management of Abram's growing assets. The Bible text states that Abram was "very rich in livestock, silver, gold" (v. 2) and that he had a private, trained security force of 300+ men (14:14). His growing possessions and responsibilities were plenty to handle. But his nephew Lot also had a growing portfolio of assets, and the area they were all trying to occupy just wasn't sustainable for the entire group anymore. The family enterprise had grown to a point where the most practical, common-sense action was for Abram and Lot to spread out for more fertile land. Lot selfishly chose the best for his operation, lured by the opportunities of city life (v. 12). And Abram graciously navigated the situation and allowed Lot to have his way. After all, he had personally experienced God's clear leading along the way, and so he demonstrated faith once again for God to provide.

God's earlier command, "Go from your country" (12:1), was then realized when Yahweh commanded Abram to "lift up your eyes and look" (13:14) at the land God had promised to give him. God was faithful to His promise, and Abram was beginning to see the vision play out before his very eyes.

Meanwhile, as a resident of Sodom, Lot found himself in the middle of a geo-political nightmare. A coalition of four kings rose up against five other kings, and the cities of Sodom and Gomorrah were captured, along with Lot, his family, and all of his possessions (14:1-12). Abram received news of the situation and deployed a force of his own, in the darkness of night, to rescue Lot (14:13-16). Blood indeed is thicker than water.

When the dust of the battle had settled, there was an incident where Abram was approached in a valley by two different kings (14:17-24). One, Melchizedek the king of Salem, represented goodness and righteousness, provided Abram with some simple bread and wine and called upon El Elyon ("God Most High"). He was focused on God, the Giver of the food, and in turn, Abram blessed Melchizedek with a tenth of all his possessions. This is the first mention of a tithe in the Bible, a concept and practice that will be developed in subsequent lessons in this book.

The other leader, the king of Sodom, tried to negotiate with Abram, suggesting Abram take possessions as his spoils and allow the king to have all the people. It was a businesslike offer for sure, but one that would ultimately jeopardize the vision and call Yahweh had given Abram. He prioritized the long-term over the immediate and would continue to be blessed as a result.

REFLECT + ACT

» It's one thing to be blessed by God, but another to steward the blessing. When God gives you money, possessions (e.g. car, house, clothes), intellectual capacity, relationships, and more–He desires for you to manage and steward those gifts well. It's possible God hasn't "blessed" you in a particular way or area because you haven't demonstrated faithful stewardship of what you have now. Are you wise with the resources God has provided you with right now? How do you spend your money, your abilities, your discretionary time? Maybe you desire greater influence but aren't faithfully pouring into and impacting those right around you. Take some time to think about this and consider sharing your thoughts with a trusted friend or advisor.

» It shouldn't be overstated, but there is something to the way Abram not only handled the strife with Lot and his herdsmen but also negotiated with the kings of Sodom and Salem. He wasn't short-sighted. He was mindful of the broader context and implications of how he responded. Abram valued God's long-term calling, and in the end stuck to it when faced with situations where he could

have benefited right away. We live in an immediacy-driven culture that idolizes instant gratification because "we deserve it." "YOLO,"[14] is what the world says. And this is why it is so important for you and me to live with purpose and intention each day and remain committed to what God has called us to do.

PRAYER

God Most High, Possessor of heaven and earth, You are faithful. I am reminded that in the midst of Abram's mistakes and challenges, You remained committed to Your promise, to the vision You had for him and those that would follow. You haven't called me to be the "father of the nations," but You have called me to know You, obey Your word, and point others to You along the way. You have blessed me in so many ways. Help me even today to be mindful of and impacted by Your faithfulness to me. I want to steward the blessings You have granted me. I want to know and be committed to my calling and live a purposeful and intentional life. But I need Your grace and power to do so. Help me today, I pray. Amen.

[14] = You Only Live Once.

ON WEALTH AND SUCCESS

Read: Genesis 15:1; 22:14; 24:1-4; 24:12; 24:26-27; 25:5; 25:11; 26:12-16; 26:24-25; 26:28 (3-4 minutes)

And Isaac sowed in that land and reaped in the same year a hundredfold. The Lord blessed him, and the man became rich, and gained more and more until he became very wealthy. He had possessions of flocks and herds and many servants, so that the Philistines envied him.

DISCUSS + MEDITATE

Soon after the rescue of Lot and the negotiations with the kings of Salem and Sodom, Yahweh met with Abram in a vision and exhorted him not to fear, but rather to rest in the fact that Yahweh Himself would be his defense and protection (15:1). Yahweh changed Abram's[15] name to Abraham and promised him a son (chapter 17). Abraham interceded on behalf of Sodom, which had become increasingly wicked (chapter 18). Lot, who was then "sitting in the gate of Sodom," had to be rescued once again to avoid God's judgment (chapter 19). After a precarious arrangement with a ruler named Abimelech, God intervened (chapter 20). True to His promise, God did, in fact, provide an heir to Abraham and Sarah by giving them their son Isaac (chapter 21). After Isaac had developed into an adolescent, Yahweh tested Abraham's faith by commanding him to sacrifice his son. Abraham passed the test and commemorated the lesson by naming that location Yahweh Yireh, which literally meant, "Yahweh will see to it" (22:14).

After Sarah passed away (chapter 23), Abraham began to look to the future and made some tangible decisions in order to preserve his vision and legacy. He sent his oldest servant on a mission to secure a bride for Isaac, a trip marked with God's providential guidance and provision– "Yahweh saw to it." The servant prayed for the success of the mission (24:12) and when he saw that everything fell into place according to God's plan, he worshiped Yahweh, honored his employer, and then thanked God for working in his own life (24:26-27). The mission was a success.

Before Abraham passed away, the text states that he gave all that he had to Isaac (25:5) and that "God blessed Isaac his son" (25:11). And Isaac worked hard to steward the blessing and the promise that had now been passed down to him, so much so that he too became "rich, and gained more and more until he became very wealthy" (25:12-13). Isaac amassed so much wealth that some of the surrounding nations not only envied him, became intimidated by him and began to make things very difficult for him in that region. But God intervened once again and brought about relative peace and calm for Isaac. God exhorted him with the same promise He had given

---

[15]Abram ("exalted father") changed to Abraham ("father of many nations")

to his father: "do not fear" (25:24). Isaac would need this reminder in dealing with his own heirs–the topic of our next lesson.

REFLECT + ACT

» Fear can be such a debilitating mental and emotional reality and can manifest itself in a variety of ways. Fear can cause us not to delegate when we should. Fear often leads to perfectionism and over-bearing attempts to control situations. Fear can develop into inaction or passivity. And ultimately, fear can rob us of experiencing God's blessing. Where do you need courage today? One of the greatest promises in all of the Bible is God's promise that He is with us. Take a moment even now to write down some of your specific fears and be reminded of God's active presence and help in your life.

» Reflect also on the future. What steps have you taken to pass God's blessing to someone else, to the next generation? Who are you mentoring right now? Which people can you begin pouring into in ways that transfer not only financial wealth but also a wealth of knowledge and instruction about how to live a life that's wise–that is not wasted and that honors God? This does not happen naturally. You must be intentional with this type of investment.

» Notice the pattern exemplified in Abraham's servant and how he processed the success of his mission (24:26-27): he thanked God, he honored his employer, and then he focused on himself. Success in any venture or sphere has a way of inflating us. But if we are men and women of God, success has the ability to humble us. How have you seen this play out in your own life?

» There's a helpful reminder in these passages that increased wealth can often lead to increased troubles and challenges. This was true for Abraham and for Isaac. Wealth can create conflict or generate envy in others, especially in those closest to us, and often by fault of our own. But it is something to be aware of. How you handle and manage wealth can also be a testimony to others of God's blessing in your life: Abimelech, his advisor, and his commander testified about Isaac, "We see plainly that the Lord has been with you" (25:28). If God blesses you with increased wealth, use it to be a blessing to others and point them to further trust in Him.

PRAYER

O Lord God, You indeed are my Shield, and You are with me. You are Yahweh Yireh, the One Who "sees to it" and makes a way. Help me to live and work today with Your presence and Your promises in mind. I want to be quick to give You praise when I experience success or material blessing, and I want this to be a testimony to those around me from my generation to the next. I'm at Your mercy. Amen.

INSTANT VS. DELAYED GRATIFICATION

Read: Genesis 25:29-34; 27:34-36; 28:1-5; 31:41-42 (3-4 minutes)
But he said, "Your brother came deceitfully, and he has taken away your blessing." Esau said, "Is he not rightly named Jacob? For he has cheated me these two times. He took away my birthright, and behold, now he has taken away my blessing."

DISCUSS + MEDITATE

At the age of sixty, Isaac and Rebekah gave birth to twin boys, Jacob and Esau. Even from birth there was conflict between them and their eventual family trees. In one instance, Jacob (whose name meant "take by the heel, cheater") convinced his slightly older brother Esau to sell his birthright in exchange for a bowl of porridge (25:29-34). In that culture the birthright was the position as head of the family and resulted in a double share of the family estate. So this was no small trade. In this moment Jacob took advantage of his brother's weakened state and flippant disposition. Esau showed no concern for his future, choosing rather to give in to instant gratification.

In another situation we see Jacob seizing a formal blessing from his father and thus cheating his brother once again. The patriarchal blessing in that culture was designed to shape the future of the one who received the blessing, much like the birthright. Isaac completely broke down when he found out about his son's deception (27:33), and Esau was filled with hatred and rage to the point where he wanted to kill his brother (27:41). After this point, Esau appears to live a profane and

unbridled existence, character qualities that were passed down to his children and grandchildren. Even in the midst of these family sins, however, God remained faithful to His promises to Abraham and to Isaac sovereignly continued to orchestrate the circumstances of their lives.

Fleeing from his brother and equipped with a new aim and fresh blessing from his father, Jacob went to live with his uncle Laban (chapter 28). During these years the deceiver ultimately met his match on more than one occasion. Laban was a man who demonstrated notable business acumen, yet also leveraged his daughters in his covetous scheme. Jacob ended up serving Laban for fourteen years in order to marry two of his daughters and served another six years to obtain animals. Consequently, Jacob's twenty years of drudgery, discipline, and tenacity paid off well for Laban, as Jacob noted: "For you had little before I came, and it has increased abundantly, and the Lord has blessed you wherever I turned" (30:30).

Jacob built his wealth over a long period of time, challenged by Laban's deceit multiple times. After one final dispute, Jacob fled Laban and took with him his two wives and children and possessions, along with a few other sentimental items of Laban's. It is interesting to note, though, that Jacob saw God's clear leading during his entire experience with Laban: "If the God of my father, the God of Abraham and the Fear of Isaac, had not been on my side, surely now you would have sent me away empty-handed. God saw my affliction and the labor of my hands" (31:42). Yes, Jacob labored and served his uncle, but ultimately he experienced divine intervention and prosperity. God chastened Jacob's pride and challenged his tenacity. God also purged self-sufficiency from his will to win, attain, and obtain, and God redirected Jacob's love to God Himself.

REFLECT + ACT

» We live and work in a society that values, even idolizes, speed and instantaneous results. Take a moment to look back on your life and the many decisions you have made. Can you think of any examples where you made a decision based on the short-term benefit or based on instant gratification? What was the situation, and did you experience any negative consequences as a result? I made an ill-informed investment once in a startup that, looking back, was based more on the quick (12-month term) 20% return I was positioned to gain. In the end, it was too good to be true. The owner of the company misappropriated my investment, along with that of many others'. Stewarding and growing the resources God has entrusted to us is more about the long view, delaying gratification in the immediate for a greater return in the future.

» A very popular belief in modern business culture is a repackaging of the ancient, Eastern concept of karma, the consequence of past actions. Ultimately, karma has to do with rebirth or reincarnation, but the term has more broadly come to mean "good things happen to those who do good and bad things happen to those who think or do bad things." Karma isn't a biblical concept, regardless of how prevalent this belief has become in business and pop culture. You and I, like Jacob, aren't the sum of all of our actions. Sure, there are positive and negative consequences for decisions we make. But through it all, God is in control and orchestrating the circumstances of our lives. Others may deceive and wrong us, yet God, our heavenly Father, uses that hurt to strengthen and grow us. God is more than capable of intervening in our lives, even when we make stupid, short-sighted decisions. He is able to right the wrongs when we have been conned or deceived in our business dealings. God is sovereign, not the nebulous universe that "experts" today tell us to "speak into."[16] Take comfort in His providential care and involvement in your life.

PRAYER

Sovereign God, thank You that You are in control. Help me grow today in learning how to make decisions that aren't based on immediate gratification. I want to live a life that is strategic and intentional—one that is wise—not one based on the moment or what's popular in the culture around me. I want to focus on how I can be faithful to You and to those within my sphere over a long period of time. Amen.

[16]This is based on the New Age belief and pseudoscience known as the Law of Attraction where positive thoughts attract positive results and negative thoughts yield negative results. This is not a biblical teaching.

HUMAN SUCCESS & DIVINE SOVEREIGNTY

Read: Genesis 39:1-23; 50:15-21 (3-4 minutes)
As for you, you meant evil against me, but God meant it for good, to bring it about that many people should be kept alive, as they are today.

DISCUSS + MEDITATE

The final chapters of Genesis focus on God's providence in the life of Jacob's son Joseph. The Bible text we read today highlights the preference Israel (Jacob's new name) had for Joseph and the ensuing hatred that favoritism triggered amongst the rest of the brothers (chapter 37). After being implicated in one of Joseph's dreams, the brothers conspired to get rid of him, ultimately selling him as a slave. Joseph ended up miles and cultures away in Egypt, in the direct service of a very influential man named Potiphar. Yet through it all, God was quietly at work behind the scenes. "The LORD was with Joseph, and he became a successful man" (39:2). Joseph further found favor with his boss and was given greater responsibility. With his good looks, freedom from supervision, and a rapid rise to a position of influence, Joseph became the target of direct, repeated temptation of a sexual nature from none other than his boss's wife.

Equipped with loyalty to his boss and a proper fear of God, Joseph refused, which triggered a setup from Potiphar's wife. She lied and framed Joseph, and he ended up in prison (39:8-23). But Yahweh was still present with Joseph and caused him to have favor with those in prison. God directly used another inmate to eventually secure Joseph's release and an appointment with the Pharaoh himself. The LORD gave Joseph specific wisdom to interpret the Pharaoh's dreams and predict the future. As a result, the ruler trusted Joseph to lead the entire nation of Egypt into a historic contingency plan—storing up grain during the plentiful years (41:33-36). After seven years of excellent harvests, everything played out as God had predicted. During a regional famine for the next seven years, surrounding people groups journeyed to Egypt for food, including Joseph's brothers, the same ones who thirteen years prior had sold him into slavery.

After some time had passed, during which Joseph tested his brothers and ensured the wellbeing of his father Jacob, Joseph finally revealed his true identity. Joseph had the authority and every right to enact revenge on his brothers, yet he chose forgiveness. He could have sent them to prison or had them put to death, but relied upon Yahweh to right the wrongs. Joseph emphatically testified, "God sent me before you to preserve life... God sent me... not you but God... God has made me lord of all Egypt" (45:5-9).

REFLECT + ACT

» The concept of being "self-made" is very popular in today's culture. We have all heard stories of people who started with nothing and went on to become an overnight success a transformation that they attributed to being "self made". The implication is that they did not really need anyone's help to achieve success and that they essentially relied only on themselves. Practically, we know that no one truly achieves success on their own. Biblically speaking, this is certainly not the case. Joseph attributed his success to divine sovereignty–God's intentional direction and presence in his life. Take a moment to reflect on this for your life. To what or to whom do you attribute your successes up to this point? How has God worked to help you achieve or prosper?

» This text further highlights the reality of temptation, particularly sexual temptation. In our society today, which has become increasingly sexualized, temptation is almost certain where there is money, success, and power. Hollywood and pop culture have glamourized and normalized this trio. Yet, this temptation does not have to define or defeat a child of God. Temptation to sexual sin can often slowly creep in, with small compromises developing here or there over time. But it can also smack you right in the face when you least expect it. Perhaps you should take some time to open up with a trusted friend or advisor to discuss specific temptations that you are currently facing. Ask God to give you the humility and courage to take decisive steps to avoid sin in this area. This may especially be needed if you are unsupervised after work or travel on business trips. God can give grace to honor Him in how we handle the various temptations that come our way.

» For further soul work dealing with temptation, consider reading John Piper's short book, *Living In The Light: Money, Sex & Power* (2016).[17]

» Consider the contingency planning that occurs in today's Bible text. One of the tangible results of God's presence in Joseph's life was the provision of extraordinary wisdom in his leadership and economic policies, particularly in planning for the future. This principle has direct implications for practices such as saving and investing, not only for you personally but also for your family and organizations you serve. What might Joseph's example mean for you and your financial planning? Take a few minutes to write some of those implications down.

PRAYER

Sovereign God, thank You for this reminder once again through Joseph's life that You are in control and are providentially leading in my life. How quickly I forget this and try to live my life on my own, as if I am self-made. Help me even today to look for Your hand guiding me in the work that You have called me to do. Help me rest in your strength and presence as I face various temptations. I want to honor You. Amen.

[17]https://www.desiringgod.org/books/living-in-the-light.

DELEGATE OR DIE

Read: Exodus 18:1-27 (4-5 minutes)

You and the people with you will certainly wear yourselves out, for the thing is too heavy for you. You are not able to do it alone.

DISCUSS + MEDITATE

We now consider the book of Exodus, which highlights God's fulfillment of His promise to Abraham to make of him and his descendants into a great nation. Exodus also records the history of deliverance for God's people–Jacob's family, called Israel or the Israelites, their entering the Promised Land, and the binding of Israel in a covenant. The first chapter points out that, "the people of Israel were fruitful and increased greatly" (1:7). But a new king came into power who saw these people and their fruitfulness as a threat. So, he began to treat them harshly. The people of God had lived in Egypt for 430 years by now, and this new king was intent on making their lives very difficult.

But God provided a deliverer–Moses (chapter 2). Now more than sixty years removed from Joseph, God preserved Moses' life to be raised in Egypt so that he might advocate and intercede for the people of God before the king. After a series of supernatural plagues, the Pharaoh finally let the Israelites go, freeing from their bondage (chapters 5-12). God led them via a pillar of cloud and fire (chapter 13), miraculously helping them cross the Red Sea (chapter 14), and providing food and water (chapters 16-17). At this point in the book of Exodus, the Israelites were a large group of people–camping in a wilderness and trying to head to the land that God had promised. They weren't slaves anymore, but everyday life was still very challenging.

In chapter 18, we read about Moses' father-in-law Jethro. He not only believed in and followed Yahweh, the one true God, but also gave Moses some sage leadership advice. While Jethro was visiting Moses in the camp, he observed Moses' work, hearing and judging various disputes between the people from morning until evening (v.13). He then asked Moses why he chose to do that job "alone" (separated or isolated). He challenged Moses on this approach, saying it was not good and could result in a breakdown–Moses would soon get burnt out, Jethro cautioned, if he single-handedly tried to keep up this pace (18:17-18). Jethro described Moses' lack of delegation as "heavy" (like a weight) and then proceeded to outline for him a more effective management framework.

Jethro first advised Moses to choose other men who were "able" (strong and efficient), who feared God, who were "trustworthy" (faithful or reliable), and who hated bribes (unjust gain) (18:21). Once Moses had identified men who met these qualifications, he could organize them to oversee small groups of Israelites, segmented by thousands, hundreds, fifties, etc. In this system, assistants would be able to help Moses shoulder the burden of leading the people and in the process, these helpers would develop as leaders themselves (18:22). Jethro also suggested that Moses teach the new leaders to use discernment between minor issues they could handle on their own and major issues that would warrant Moses' immediate attention. And what was the result of this kind of organizational management? Verse 23 states that if Moses reorganized in this way, he would be able to "endure," and the people would experience "peace" (satisfaction). Identifying and employing other leaders would ultimately lead to longevity and sustainability for Moses so that he could continue to focus on the mission God had called him to do.

REFLECT + ACT

» Maybe you've tried to delegate before, but that person ended up not being "able" or "trustworthy," and so you've just decided to go it alone. Maybe you struggle with fear and think about all the worst-case scenarios if you brought others around you to carry some of the load. What has been your experience with delegation? Or what areas of your life and work could be assigned to someone else so that you can focus on your core competencies and mission? Consider talking to a mentor or advisor to help you in this area.

» When done effectively and consistently, delegation can be a tangible tool to develop leaders around you. If this is a challenge for you, I encourage you to read Jordan Raynor's book *Redeeming Your Time: 7 Biblical Principles for Being Purposeful, Present & Wildly Productive* (2021).[18]

» In terms of organizational management, recruiting, retention, and starting or building a business, I'd like to recommend another helpful book, *Traction: Get a Grip on Your Business* (Wickman, 2011)[19]. In this highly acclaimed book, Wickman systematically outlines six components that make up what he calls the Entrepreneurial Operating System® (EOS). One component focuses on attracting the right people for the right seats.

PRAYER

God, the One Who will fight for us like You did for the Israelites, thank You for Your Word. Thank You once again for preserving it so that I can read it today and be changed by it. I am reminded of Your faithful leading of and provision for Your people throughout the ages, especially in how You preserved, called, and used Moses. Thank You for opening the eyes of his father-in-law Jethro to see that You are greater than all gods. His insight and advice regarding delegation is relevant for me today with my work. Help me to process this lesson so that I might be a more effective leader for Your glory. Amen.

[18]https://jordanraynor.com.
[19]https://www.eosworldwide.com/traction-book.

THE DANGER OF DESIRE

Read: Exodus 20:1-17 (2-3 minutes)
You shall not covet your neighbor's house; you shall not covet your neighbor's wife, or his male servant, or his female servant, or his ox, or anything that is your neighbor's.

DISCUSS + MEDITATE

After Jethro's advice, the people of God remained in the wilderness of Sinai. This was now three months after their deliverance from Egypt. Yahweh was in the process of preserving them and setting them apart from the pagan people groups around them. He referred to His people as a "treasured possession" and a "holy nation" (19:5-6). Yahweh desired that His people would pursue moral excellence as a means of reflecting His own character to a watching world. So, the narrative of Exodus shifts now in chapters 20-31 to focus on this specific covenant community and the ways that they should worship and work together.

Exodus 20 records perhaps the most well-known set of instructions given by God–the Ten Commandments (or Ten Words). Like a national constitution, these words from God outlined key instructions for how this new people of Yahweh should interact with Him and with others to create a society that existed for God's glory and the good of all.

The first word addressed God's exclusive claim for service and allegiance from His people ("You shall have no other gods before me" 20:3). In a culture that possessed and worshiped multiple national, family, and personal gods, Yahweh demanded supreme worship. To be truly separate and different, God's people could not follow any other form of divine representation. Fast-forward to chapter 32 and read about an instance where the people of God formed a golden, calf-shaped idol. There, Yahweh revealed again that He was a jealous God ("whose name is Jealous" 34:14). He alone was worthy of worship, commandment number one states.

Yahweh's fourth word reminded His people of the richness of rest ("Remember the Sabbath day, to keep it holy" 20:8). This rest day was instituted from the very beginning–we considered it in Lesson 4. Now some 2,500 years after the Garden of Eden, the people of God were to implement this day of rest as a "sign" of God's covenant with them (31:12-17). Sabbath was to be a lifestyle and mindset demonstrating that the people belonged to Yahweh and were sustained by His hand. On this side of Egypt, the weekly Sabbath was to be a means of remembering their redemption from slavery. Slaves were to be freed (21:2), and every seven years the land was not to be cultivated for a year (23:10-11). This was a pattern of work and rest.

With the tenth and final word, Yahweh instructed His people not to covet what did not belong to them, which included houses, spouses, and possessions (20:17). Coveting (wanting, craving, desiring) in general was not prohibited. However, desiring things that were not theirs was a sin. This addresses an issue of mind and heart and is connected to the first word dealing with worshiping other gods. Yahweh wanted His people to trust Him as their provider and curtail their desires for the good of the broader community.

REFLECT + ACT

» Reformer John Calvin wrote, "Man's nature, so to speak, is a perpetual factory of idols"[20]. There is an attraction in every culture and society to look to other gods or sources for guidance and provision. This might look like using tarot cards to predict your future, relying on astrology, or making your intentions known to "The Universe." The business world is filled with individuals who often, like the people of Yahweh in Exodus, try to synchronize belief in God with other more tangible representations of His presence or another deity or divine representative. You and I need to be discerning and careful to not engage in these types of idolatrous beliefs and practices. True faith in God is, by definition in Scripture, exclusive ("You shall have no other gods before me" 20:3). The reality is that we can literally turn anything into another god or idol[21]. Success, sex, power, status, money, affirmation, our own bodies, religion, work–and on and on it goes. What other gods are you tempted to worship? What are you trying to include with God in your worship?

» In today's culture, the early 19th-century philosophy of manifestation (Law of Attraction) has become increasingly popular. The basic premise is that there is a universal inter-relatedness without a central deity. As a result, we can create our own reality by carefully controlling our thoughts, beliefs, and desires. This is sometimes associated with mindfulness, meditation, and visualization. What might appear on the surface as positivity has roots fixed in manifesting things or experiences that we don't currently have, the essence of a covetous heart. Marketing and sales experts might say the reason you aren't successful yet is because you haven't attracted or manifested success. Be careful with this kind of thinking and with practices such as vision boards, which can be helpful in setting goals, but often are just a means of highlighting the idols of our heart.

PRAYER

Holy God, Whose name is Jealous, forgive me for the thoughts and plans of my covetous, idol-making heart. I desperately need Your strength and presence to help me identify all of the ways I am prone to create other gods. I need discernment to filter all of the messaging that says I can create my own reality and satisfy the desires of my heart. How godless that belief system is! I want to trust in and worship You and You alone. I want to regularly rest in You. Amen.

[20]*Institutes of the Christian Religion.*
[21]Consider reading Keller's book, *Counterfeit Gods* (2009). https://timothykeller.com/books/counterfeit-gods.

GOD'S ECONOMY

Read: Exodus 22:21-27 (1-2 minutes)
If you lend money to any of my people with you who is poor, you shall not be like a moneylender to him, and you shall not exact interest from him.

DISCUSS + MEDITATE

The broader context of this lesson covers forty years of Israel's history, from Sinai (chapter 20) to Leviticus, Numbers, and up to the edge of the Promised Land. God outlined through Moses what holiness and wholeheartedness should look like among His people and how they should act toward each other in the community. This was God's ideal commonwealth. God wanted His people to depend fully on Him and allow His rule to color every arena of their lives, including their possessions and money. God commanded them to not steal because that threatened the social order of the covenant community (20:15). He instituted voluntary offerings and opportunities to give financially, preserving Israel's identity socioeconomically and reminding them that He was ultimately the Owner of everything.

In Exodus chapters 23 and 35, Yahweh provided an opportunity for His people to demonstrate generosity by contributing their resources, their skills, and time to the construction of the Tabernacle, a movable tent used for meeting to worship God. There were skillful men and women in Israel, the text says, whose hearts "stirred" to serve God in these tangible ways (35:21).

They had "generous hearts" (35:5) and were moved with commitment to Yahweh and compassion for others. The Israelites did so voluntarily and willingly– they gave "freewill offerings"(35:29).

God instituted laws about the restitution of animals and property (21:33-22:15). He established feasts and festivals to periodically remind His people that He was their Redeemer and that they were His possession. He saw to it in His economy that no one owned their land and servants indefinitely. There were laws dealing with the redemption of people and property (Leviticus 25:23-34). There was also a provision that land was to remain fallow or rest during the Sabbath year ("solemn rest" 25:1-7). Yahweh instituted a system of offerings, some voluntary (burnt, grain, peace) and some required to cleanse from sin (guilt, sin) (chapters 1-7). Some offerings were to be administered daily (Numbers 28:1-8), some each Sabbath (28:9-10), some monthly (28:11-15), and some yearly at Passover (28:16-25). These were all regular means to cultivate personal holiness and draw closer to God.

There was a natural connection between personal piety and how God's people were to treat each other, especially those who were materially poor. Yahweh himself said He hears the cries of the poor (Ex. 22:23, 27) and that He is "compassionate" (22:27). He wanted His people to do and be the same. He didn't want them to charge interest when lending money (22:25). He wanted those who had fields and vineyards to leave the wheat and grapes that had fallen during the harvesting process so that the poor and visitors could have food to eat (Lev.19:9-10; 23:22). God further wanted His people to show kindness to the poor and visitors by providing them homes and food without charging them (25:35-46). They were to be responsible for their fellow man and help the needy and strangers.

REFLECT + ACT
» Think about these three primary results from God's ideal commonwealth:

» *Greater dependence on God*—Repeatedly, God reminded His people that He was God and was the One Who had redeemed them from slavery in Egypt. He had to remind them because they easily forgot. The same tendency is true for us today. God ultimately wants our hearts. He called for a Sabbath year so that His people would learn to trust in Him for their provision. He calls us to trust Him in a similar way. He wants us to be committed to Him and make His name great throughout the earth. He wants us to voluntarily and regularly give from a heart that is willing and free.

» *Restraint against greed*—By instituting seasons where land and servants could be returned and fields would remain fallow, God provided a built-in system to restrain people from excessive wealth accumulation. He asked people to contribute their time, money, and skills to create a place for worship, giving them the opportunity to focus on serving Him and not merely their own needs. It's difficult for greed to take root and grow in our hearts when we are constantly looking for ways to help those around us. This is true for us individually, for our families, for our organizations that we are a part of, and the broader socio-political community we are connected to.

» *Social stability*—The causes of material poverty are multifaceted today, much in the same way that they were for the people of Israel. Ultimately, poverty is rooted in broken relationships–with God, each other, and the rest of creation. The rule of God in every aspect of life should have a stabilizing effect on families and companies and communities. Responsibility, kindness, and compassion are all hallmarks of holiness and means of restoring the brokenness in and around us.[22]

PRAYER
God, the One Who brought Your people out of the land of Egypt and gave them the land of Canaan, You are my God. I am your possession, and You own everything. Help me reflect your ideal commonwealth by depending on You, by turning from greed and embracing willing generosity. I want to limit my accumulation so that I am free to give to others and to Your work. I need Your rule to be evident in my life and work today. Amen.

[22]Consider reading *When Helping Hurts* by Corbett & Fikkert (2012), which provides a biblical framework of poverty, adapted from Myers' book, *Walking with the Poor* (2011).

THE DANGERS OF WEALTH & BLESSING

17

Read: Deuteronomy 8:1-20 (3-4 minutes)

Beware lest you say in your heart, "My power and the might of my hand have gotten me this wealth." You shall remember the Lord your God, for it is he who gives you power to get wealth.

DISCUSS + MEDITATE

The book of Deuteronomy forms a treaty of sorts, a covenant renewal document between God and Israel. As the people of Israel grouped on the plains of Moab, waiting to cross over into Canaan (the Promised Land), Moses once again imparts wide-ranging principles and laws from God, covering all areas of life (e.g. economics, leadership, property). Understanding and following these laws would form the basis of God's kingdom on earth, specifically describing how God's people should love Him and each other. Ultimately, Moses wanted to remind the people at the end of his leadership term that God was faithful (7:9) and that God demanded that His people obey His word and remain different from the unbelieving people that surrounded them (7:6).

In this final sermon, Moses warned these people to not forget Yahweh, saying it at least four times (4:9; 6:12; 8:11; 8:14). He knew they were about to enter a land overflowing with blessings. They were about to inherit cities and houses that they didn't build, enjoy vineyards they didn't plant, and utilize wells that they didn't dig (6:10-15). Additionally, these nomadic people were going to come face-to-face with many idols made of silver and gold, and Moses knew they would immediately be tempted to "go after other gods" (6:14). He knew they would be tempted by covetousness (7:25)—that they could become complacent with all the abundance and develop a mindset and lifestyle of self-sufficiency. *Full bellies. New homes. Accumulation. Forgetfulness.*

As a result, Moses warned them multiple times to "take care" (4:9; 11:6), to "watch yourselves very carefully" like a night watchman (4:15), to "keep your soul diligently" (4:9), and not to allow their hearts "to be lifted up" (8:14). To maintain a careful commitment to God would require diligence and vigilance. Moses knew that once they began to experience this newfound wealth, many would begin to believe it was actually the result of their own doing. He warned, "Beware lest you say in your heart, 'My power and the might of my hand have gotten me this wealth.' You shall remember the LORD your God, for it is he who gives you power to get wealth" (8:17-18). God's people, Moses said, were going to be tempted to rely on their own strength and wisdom and in the process conclude that they no longer needed Yahweh.

In the end, Yahweh would bless them because He, for generations, had said He would. He was, and is, "the faithful God who keeps covenant and steadfast love" (7:9). He was, and is, jealous for His people (4:24; 6:15) and merciful (4:31). Yahweh commanded them to love Him with their entire being—*heart* (intellect), *soul* (will or essence), *might* (capacity or power) (6:4-5). This love was to be all-encompassing, inclusive of the full impact and weight of their relational, intellectual, and financial capital. Total obedience. Demonstration of this love would mean obedience to God's words. His laws were most important: the spiritual food that they had experienced was to have greater priority than their physical food (8:3 "man does not live by bread alone").

Love and obedience. Wholeheartedness and *holiness. Diligence and vigilance.* These were the means provided to avoid forgetting the LORD or trying to live a self-sufficient life.

REFLECT + ACT
» Consider these practical ways to be careful so that you do not forget the LORD in your daily life and work. These are some tangible suggestions to help you avoid covetousness, complacency, and self-sufficiency and live a life that demonstrates love for the LORD and others.

» Spend as much or more time each day digesting spiritual food as you do with physical food. When you do eat actual food,

make it a habit to thank God for providing it. Set aside a regular time or times each day to read the Bible, perhaps in conjunction with your regular mealtimes. Consider incorporating Scripture memory, Bible reading, and prayer into your family mealtimes or work lunches and dinners. Set a goal to pray for the same length of time that you spend physically exercising or working out.

» Keep a journal (a physical notebook or phone app) where you can archive how God has demonstrated His faithfulness to you and provided for you.

» Find someone other than your spouse or significant other who can touch base with you weekly to encourage you in taking care and keeping your soul. Get in the habit of asking people how their soul is while also asking for updates on work, family, etc.

» Consider, if you haven't already, forming or joining a small group of other believers from your church or within your organization where you all can regularly help each other minimize temptation and maximize holiness to the Lord.

PRAYER
God, You are faithful and loyal to Your promises. I feel the weight of these demands to be holy and to love You with my whole being. You have blessed me in so many ways and yet in that blessing I have often forgotten You and lived in my own strength and wisdom. Forgive me. I want to grow in my love for You. In Jesus' name, amen.

SOFT HEARTS & OPEN HANDS

18

Read: Deuteronomy 28:1-15 (2-3 minutes)
And the LORD will make you abound in prosperity…

DISCUSS + MEDITATE

After challenging the people of Israel to take care of and keep their souls so that they wouldn't become self-sufficient and forget the LORD, Moses continued his final words to them regarding laws of interpersonal relationships. Again, he was trying to prepare them for what life would be like once they crossed into Canaan, the Promised Land. They were about to experience unprecedented blessing and prosperity, and he wanted to make sure everyone benefited and understood God's reasons for these commands: they were to be "holy to himself [God]" (28:9) and in their thriving, they were to show all the peoples of the earth "that you are called by the name of the LORD" (28:10). God fulfilling His promises and blessing His people were means of displaying His glory and superiority over all the other gods.

Moses reminded the people that God was not partial and cared deeply for the vulnerable and marginalized in their society (orphans, widows, visitors, strangers) (10:17-19). He outlined various tithes (14:22-29), reminding them of the importance of both dependence on God and generosity. Moses highlighted the provisions of the sabbatical year once again as a means of caring for the poor and those passing through their region as travelers (15:1-11). The ideal in God's economy was that there be no poor, especially from among the people of Israel (15:4). But the reality was that there would always be those at the bottom of the socioeconomic pyramid because of the lack of faithfulness in living out God's instructions. As a result, the people were to demonstrate a softness of heart and an openness of hand when it came to the poor among them. They weren't to look down upon the poor as inferior, but were to "give freely" and "open wide your hand" (15:10-11).

Moses gave final reminders that the people were not to charge interest on loans to their fellow Israelites (23:19). If a loan went into default and the only collateral the debtor had was their cloak (think sleeping bag), then it could be taken but needed to be returned each night so that they wouldn't get too cold (24:10-13). The dignity of the debtor was to be maintained. Wages were to be paid daily so that the workers had means to eat and get basic necessities (24:14-15). There was to be honesty in business dealings, such as bartering and buying or selling commodities (25:13-16). And from the first and best of their harvests, Israelites were to set aside a portion directly to the LORD (26:2,10).

Why all of these rules regarding money especially? The way God's people treated each other was a direct reflection on Yahweh Himself. How they handled their possessions would reflect what was truly in their hearts. And ultimately, God wanted His people to experience the blessings that came from obedience. Deuteronomy 28 is devoted to the contrasts between blessing and curses, obedience and disobedience. God's desire was to make His people "abound in prosperity" (28:11) by opening "his good treasury" (28:12), but only if His people obeyed all of the instructions that were given to them through Moses. When they disobeyed, and they did often, they were subject to curses (28:20), including the loss of physical health and material prosperity, mental instability (28:28), lack of success in everything they set out to accomplish (28:29), and unfulfilled plans (28:30). *Frustration. Confusion. Lack of fulfillment.* God was serious with His people. He wanted their hearts, and He wanted their devotion. And He didn't want His people taking their prosperity for granted and thinking it was a result of their own doing.

REFLECT + ACT

» God still delights to bless His people today, often with material prosperity. Wealth is not guaranteed, and we cannot assume that those who experience prosperity have obeyed the Lord in all aspects of their lives. So, we need to be careful with how we view material blessing. However, as a general principle, God will bless His people in a variety of ways when they obey Him. He also has His ways of disciplining His children when we choose to go our own way and sin against Him. Sometimes, God simply leaves us with the natural consequences of our choices. Or He can allow our plans to be frustrated and unfulfilled. What are some times when you believe you have experienced this type of discipline from God as a result of your disobedience? What took place mentally or circumstantially to bring you back to Him?

» How do you typically view poor people, perhaps even those who are materially poor within your church or workplace? Do you look at them grudgingly? Do you consider them inferior in any way? Do you try to take advantage of them? Reflect on these questions and pray, asking God to forgive you of ways you have not been reflecting His heart for the poor.

» As footnoted in Lesson 16, the book *When Helping Hurts* articulates a biblically based framework concerning the root causes of poverty and its alleviation.[23]

PRAYER

God, like the children of Israel, I am also called by You to be holy, to demonstrate that I have been called by Your name. You indeed have blessed me in so many ways, and I beg You to continue to bless me in every way. But I want to be the person You desire me to be. I want my heart and life to reflect Yours, especially in my care for the most vulnerable of people around me. Forgive me for my self-seeking ways. Forgive me for my lack of concern. I never want to experience Your discipline, Your leaving me to my own devices because I have turned from you. Help me, God. I am at your mercy. Amen.

[23]https://chalmers.org/resources/books/.

MEDITATE FOR SUCCESS

Read: Joshua 1:1-9 (1-2 minutes)

This Book of the Law shall not depart from your mouth, but you shall meditate on it day and night, so that you may be careful to do according to all that is written in it. For then you will make your way prosperous, and then you will have good success.

DISCUSS + MEDITATE

The book of Deuteronomy brings the first five books of the Bible (called the Pentateuch) to a close with a description of the transition of leadership from Moses to his assistant Joshua. Moses at this point was 120 years old, with increased limitations on his capacity to lead. In a solemn assembly, he charged the people and his successor to "be strong and courageous" because God would be going before them into the Promised Land (Deut. 31:6-8). Yahweh Himself also exhorted Joshua not to fear (31:23).

Joshua would never be able to replace Moses in the impact of his leadership, but he would be used by Yahweh in substantial ways because of his preparation and devotion. Joshua had been one of the twelve spies chosen by Moses to scope out the Promised Land for forty days and bring back examples of the fruit there and feedback about what Israel might be up against in terms of a future conquest. Only Joshua and Caleb—just two of the twelve–provided an optimistic report, focused on Yahweh's presence and power (Numbers 13-14). As a result, Moses promised that only those two would be allowed to enter the Promised Land, and he changed Joshua's name from Hoshea to Joshua, which meant "Yahweh saves or delivers." Joshua had also served as a military leader (Ex.17) and personal assistant to Moses for many years (Ex. 33:11; Josh. 1:1).

Joshua was "full of the spirit of wisdom" (Dt. 34:9). Experience and observation over time had prepared him for this transition, and he would need that wisdom to oversee the equitable, efficient division of the Promised Land among the tribes of Israel. After Moses died, Yahweh assured Joshua of His constant presence and leading in his life: "I will be with you. I will not leave you or forsake you... Do not be frightened, and do not be dismayed, for the LORD your God is with you wherever you go" (Josh. 1:5, 9). Because of God's promise, Joshua developed a resolve in his character and leadership as he assumed the role of theocratic administrator. Yahweh provided a formula for success in all of Joshua's endeavors, success that was more spiritual in nature.

Success from the LORD's perspective wasn't about administrative skills or military genius; it was more about devotion to Him. *Knowing and obeying*. And the primary means of knowing Yahweh was through His Word. He wanted Joshua, and subsequently the people, to be rooted in the Law so much that it was the content of their continuous meditation: "You shall meditate on it day and night." This meaning of meditate was to audibly recite truths about God, His works, and His Law. This daily commitment and devotion leads to success in godly life endeavors and to spiritual prosperity. And Israel did experience success. The people of God under Joshua's leadership crossed the Jordan River (Josh.3) and ate of the fruit of the land of Canaan (5:12). They conquered the city of Jericho (chapter 6) and "the LORD was with Joshua, and his fame was in all the land" (6:27). God was faithful to His promises and used Joshua as a servant to carry out His purposes in the land on behalf of His people.

REFLECT + ACT

>> Oftentimes in modern culture, strength and courage are supposedly traits we can develop by psyching ourselves up mentally or through daily affirmation routines. If I say over and over, "I am strong and confident," then I will eventually manifest those qualities and actualize them. But this approach is not godly—it can easily focus on self and bypass the true Source of strength and courage–God and His faithful presence and promises. If you have a daily morning routine and affirm anything, let it be God-centered truth. Consider developing or replacing your affirmations with statements such as, "I am loved by God"; "God will never leave me or forsake me"; "God is a Rock and I can run

to Him and be safe"; "I can be strong and courageous because my God is with me."

>> Take a moment to think again about God's formula for success—knowing and obeying. How does our culture define success, and how has that definition impacted you and your work? What changes might you need to make since success in God's eyes is defined more spiritually, more about being immersed in His Word and being faithful to apply it in our everyday lives?

>> Consider reading *The Wisdom Pyramid: Feeding Your Soul in a Post-Truth World* (McCracken, 2021).[24] This book will challenge you to increase your intake of "enduring trustworthy sources" while moderating your consumption of less reliable sources.

PRAYER
God, You are the Rock, and Your work is perfect. You are faithful to Your promises, even in spite of our repeated unbelief and sin. Thank You for how You used Moses and how You prepared Joshua for his important role. You have reminded me once again that You are always with me: You will never, ever leave me or forsake me. What amazing promises! Help me today and this week to be strong and courageous as I intentionally allow Your presence and promises to guide me. I don't need to fear what today or tomorrow might bring. Help me to become more and more a person of Your word. To the praise of Your glory. Amen.

[24]https://www.brettmccracken.com/the-wisdom-pyramid

COUNTING THE DAYS & MAKING THE DAYS COUNT

Read: Psalm 90 (2-3 minutes)
So teach us to number our days that we may get a heart of wisdom.

DISCUSS + MEDITATE

Before moving on further in Joshua and the other historical books of the Old Testament, let us consider a psalm attributed to Moses that he most likely wrote just before the events of the previous lesson. The tone of Psalm 90 is one of lament on behalf of the covenant people of Israel: lament over sin, the brevity of life, and the difficulties of life. The psalm begins with the recognition that God is a Shelter, is eternal, and is the Creator—a reference back to Genesis 1-3. He has and always will exist. It was Moses who encouraged the people that "the eternal God is your dwelling place" (Dt. 33:27). Eternity is ultimately the answer to spiritual homelessness and human rootlessness.

Verses three through eleven remind us, as spiritual heirs to God's covenant, that life is short and filled with hardships. Humbling to human pride, our length of life is compared to that of a night shift, a flood, a dream, and grass (90:4-5). Even if a human lives seventy or eighty years—or even a thousand years—it is still considered brief in comparison to God's eternality (90:4). Moses gives the sense that humanity is ever-renewed, yet ever-fading at the same time. Why is this the case? The universal

shadow of the fall of man in the Garden of Eden is cast upon all humanity: we are unified in our sin nature and in sin's consequences (90:7,9). The psalmist then asks, "Who considers the power of your anger and your wrath?" (90:11). When living for the moment, Israel wasn't considering those realities or God's presence.

Moses concludes this psalm with eight specific requests of Yahweh, requests for God to increase His people's self-awareness and intentionality throughout their short lives. In verse 12 Moses asks the LORD to teach them to number their days. The word number has the idea of counting, assigning, or prioritizing. This practice would result in awareness of the brevity of life and in wise living. In verse 13 he asks Yahweh to return and have pity on Israel in their hardships. In verse 14, perhaps writing at night, Moses looks longingly at the morning, considering the presence of God as He meets with them. He asks to be satisfied or quenched with Yahweh's loving loyalty ("lovingkindness," the idea of steadfast love), a satisfaction that would generate joy and gladness ("flourishing"). Again in verse 15 he prays that they as a covenant people would flourish ("be glad") every day of their lives. Joy in their circumstances was directly connected to their faithful embrace of their covenant with Yahweh.

In the final two verses, Moses offered three additional requests of the LORD. He desired for God's work and power to be put on display among the people and to the next generation (v.16). He also wanted God's favor and beauty to be evident in their lives while He "established" the work of their hands (v.17). The term establish has to do with arranging and directing. The term work can also mean labor, business, or occupation. Moses's prayer was for God to demonstrate His sovereign directing in the mundane affairs of their lives, especially through the work they were doing that pertained to their calling. Their work and their mindset about their work had the potential to be characterized by joy. Moses prayed that their work would result in the flourishing of each person in their community.

REFLECT + ACT

» Before being swept away in the busyness of the day, allow God to meet with you through this psalm of Moses. Allow Him to generate a more refined and sustained self-awareness in your life, making you more mindful that life indeed is very short and it needs to be lived intentionally. Take the initiative to meet with a friend or trusted advisor to help you reorient your view of how you spend your time—your minutes, hours, days, months, years.

» Consider starting or revamping a consistent morning routine that allows you to incorporate time in God's Word, in prayer

to Him, and in meditation on all He is and is doing in your life. If you practice some sort of affirmations, as discussed in the last lesson, make sure you're daily meditating on truths of the Bible. You could begin by thinking about this psalm, the words Moses wrote regarding God's eternality, life's brevity, and flourishing in our work.

» Consider reading *Don't Waste Your Life* by John Piper (2007).[25]

» Listen to "O God, Our Help in Ages Past"[26] (Isaac Watts, 1719) as well as "Psalm 90" ("Satisfy Us with Your Love") by Shane & Shane (2021)[27]. Both of these songs, one very old and one modern, are both based on this psalm.

PRAYER
Father, teach me to number my days so that I may gain a heart of wisdom. Return, O Yahweh. Have pity on me, your servant. Satisfy me each morning with Your faithful love so that I will rejoice and be glad all my days. Make me glad for as many days as You give me here on this earth. Show Your work to Your servants and even our children. Let Your favor and beauty be upon me and establish the work of my hands. Amen.

[25]https://www.desiringgod.org/books/dont-waste-your-life.
[26]Isaac Watts, O God Our Help in Ages Past (1719)
[27]Shane & Shane, Psalm 90 (2021)

CORPORATE SOLIDARITY

Read: Joshua 7:1; 7:10-26 (3-4 minutes)

And Achan answered Joshua, "Truly I have sinned against the LORD God of Israel, and this is what I did: when I saw...then I coveted them and took them"

DISCUSS + MEDITATE

Now that we've considered Psalm 90, we will pick back up with the story of Moses' successor, Joshua. As noted in devotional 19, Joshua assumed the role of theocratic administrator of Israel after Moses. In the very early days of Joshua's leadership, Yahweh reminded him that He would be with him and that success in leading the people would depend not on his administrative and military skills alone but rather on his knowing and obeying God.

And Joshua experienced success under God's leading as Israel finally crossed the Jordan River into the Promised Land (Josh. 3). After the successful crossing, the text states that Yahweh exalted Joshua in the sight of all Israel (4:14). But the people of God would face one of their first tests of faith and devotion on the other side of the Jordan in a conquest to overthrow a fortified city called Jericho, one of the oldest cities in the world.

In preparation for this battle, one in which Yahweh had already promised victory, Joshua exhorted the people to keep themselves from the "things devoted to destruction" and to make sure to take any silver and gold plunder and put it in the LORD's treasury (6:18-19). This instruction was reminiscent of the warning Moses had given the children of Israel before they entered the Promised Land. He knew they would be tempted with all of the material blessings they would immediately experience. Back in Deuteronomy 7:25-26, Moses specifically charged the people not to covet the silver and gold or allow it to ensnare them, because doing so would result in them being devoted to destruction as well.[28]

Now, in the conquest of Jericho, Yahweh was going to judge the people of Cannan as a symbolic representation of what happens when people defy His instructions. The inhabitants of this pagan city–likely a center of moon worship– would soon meet their fate as Yahweh used Joshua and his men of valor to completely and miraculously destroy Jericho.

But the thrill of victory was quickly replaced by the horrible realization that someone had indeed taken some silver, gold, and an expensive coat, and hid it all in their tent. Although it would soon come to light that a man named Achan was personally to blame, the entire nation of Israel was actually implicated and guilty

---

[28]We considered this in devotional 17: The Dangers of Wealth & Blessing

just the same. The text states, "But the people of Israel broke faith in regard to the devoted thing" (7:1), and "Israel has sinned… transgressed my covenant…they have taken…they have stolen and lied" (7:10-11).

It wasn't the amount that was stolen, even though commentators believe the coat, silver, and gold would have been the equivalent of a lifetime's worth of wages for an average worker at that time. The issue was the fact that someone took and kept even the smallest item that was supposed to either be destroyed or turned over to the treasury. It was a failure on Achan's part to believe Yahweh's Word and to rely on His generosity. It was a turning of Achan's affections towards something else.

After an investigation, the truth came out, and Achan admitted what he had done. As a result, he was devoted to destruction like the citizens of Jericho, and he was promptly and publicly stoned to death by the same people he had impacted through his greed and covetousness. Yahweh then turned from His anger, and His people were reminded that He is a holy God and that there are always consequences for transgressing His commands.

REFLECT + ACT
» This is now at least the fourth devotional where we have considered the sin of greed and covetousness. So, here's another reminder to pause and reflect on what the Lord is trying to teach us through this passage. The pattern of Achan's sin is eerily similar to that of Eve's—he saw, coveted, took. This is almost always the pattern for you and me today: We see things in ads, on billboards, on our phones,

and immediately our idolatry-prone hearts say, "I want it!" Maybe it's fame and notoriety. Maybe it's a fancier car or a second home. Maybe it's someone else's spouse. Whatever it is, our society seems to intentionally target our greed reflex— and we often give in to the temptation to covet. Let's be on the alert and be quick to confess this sin to the Lord.

» The story of Achan's sin is a weighty passage of Scripture but one that serves as a stark reminder that there are real consequences for sin. There's an old adage I remember from my childhood that says, "Sin will take you farther than you want to go, will keep you longer than you want to stay, and will cost you more than you want to pay." The consequences of sin always outlast the pleasure of it. Read that statement again! It's true, and most of us have the stories and scars to show for it. If needed, allow today's devotional to be a wake-up call, a lifeline straight to God's mercy and forgiveness.

PRAYER
Holy Father—the One Who was with Joshua and exalted him, the One Who fought for Your people and brought them into the Promised Land, the One Who is a jealous God and whose anger burned because of Achan's sin—You alone are holy. Thank you for this merciful reminder that there are tangible consequences for my sin, my self-centeredness, greed and covetous heart Help me not to lose sight of Your generous character and not to grow impatient with Your leading in my life. Help me to see the fleeting pleasures of sin and find pleasure and satisfaction in You. I am at Your mercy. Amen.

THE COMPOUND EFFECT OF COMPROMISE

Read: Joshua 23:1-16; 24:14-15 (3-4 minutes)
So the men took some of their provisions, but did not ask counsel from the LORD.

DISCUSS + MEDITATE

In the narrative of the book of Joshua, just after the events of Achan's sin, the people of Israel are preparing to conquer other people groups who lived in the land God had promised to them. Jericho was the first to fall. Chapters 9 through 12 catalog how Yahweh fought for Israel as they withstood both a six-king alliance and five-king alliance and conquered the people and lands of southern and northern Canaan. Yahweh even miraculously had the sun to stand still in order to secure Israel's victory over an Amorite alliance (chapter 10). Group after group, land after land—God was Israel's guide and fighter.

But Israel wasn't completely faithful to Yahweh. In chapter 9, a people group called the Gibeonites devised a scheme to remain in the good graces of Israel and not be destroyed like so many of the other people groups in Canaan up to that point. Joshua unwisely decided to make a treaty with them: "The men took some of their provisions, but did not ask counsel from the LORD" (9:14). Yahweh had required Israel to seek His counsel, especially in matters dealing with foreign people groups. But in this situation, they compromised and did not ask God for wisdom first.

Chapters 13 through 24 focus less on taking the land by conquest and more on receiving the land from Yahweh through allotment. God reveals Himself here as the great Landowner and Land-giver. Region by region, God systematically apportioned land to each of the twelve tribes of Israel, as He had always promised He would. But some of the tribes didn't fully follow Yahweh's instructions and experienced the consequences. Joshua 13:13 states, "Yet the people of Israel did not drive out the Geshurites or the Maacathites."

Fast-forward many years into Israel's existence: King David was opposed by the Maacathites that earlier generations had allowed to remain in the land, and David's son Absalom was born to a Geshurite princess. We don't see those future events here, but we do see multiple examples of incomplete obedience and compromise. Joshua 15:63 tells us that the tribe of Judah couldn't drive out the Jebusites. Joshua 16:10 highlights the tribe of Ephraim's failure to drive out the Canaanites at Gezer. Instead, they instead kept these enemies of Yahweh around and used them for forced labor. Joshua 17:12 tells of the western half-tribe of Manasseh and their inability to drive out the Canaanites in their region, also using them for forced labor. Over and over, the people of God chose to tolerate wickedness and use for their own benefit those God had said to destroy.

At the backdrop of this pattern of compromise and unfaithfulness is the consistent faithfulness of Yahweh. Joshua 21:43-45 serves as a summary statement of everything that had taken place but also as a thematic statement for the entire book of Joshua. Consider the amazing faithfulness of God as you read these words:

> Thus the LORD gave to Israel all the land that he swore to give to their fathers. And they took possession of it, and they settled there. And the LORD gave them rest on every side just as he had sworn to their fathers. Not one of all their enemies had withstood them, for the LORD had given all their enemies into their hands. Not one word of all the good promises that the LORD had made to the house of Israel had failed; all came to pass.

As the process of land conquest and allotment comes to an end in Joshua 23 and 24, so does the long, fruitful life of Joshua himself. With his remaining strength, the elderly Joshua exhorted the leaders and the people of Israel to be strong and obey Yahweh, to remain separate from foreign nations and their gods, to hold fast to Yahweh and His Word, and to be careful to love Him with their whole hearts. If they failed to do so, they would fall into a snare and would experience a whip and thorns until they perished (23:13). God would remain faithful, but there would be consequences if they turned from Him.

REFLECT + ACT

» We are reminded that God is to be consulted, and when we ignore Him, we do so at our own peril. Practically, we can gain God's counsel by praying, by consistently reading and studying the Bible, and by inviting other believers into our decision-making process. This is especially crucial for those of us starting or running businesses. How often do you first consult with God before making a significant business decision?

» We are also reminded of the compounding effect of compromise. You are probably familiar with the phenomenon of compounded interest and investing over time. But there is also a compounding effect when we choose to tolerate wickedness and sin in our lives. We make small compromises here and there, and before we realize it, these bad decisions have compounded and snowballed into a reality that is difficult to overcome. Allow this to be a wake-up call to you, and reassess how you do business or those whom you partner with.

PRAYER

God, the Guide of Israel and Fighter for Your people, the great Landowner and Land-giver—great is Your faithfulness! There is no shadow of turning with You. You don't change. Your compassions—they do not fail. As You have been, You forever will be. May this be the anthem of my day today and even of my life. Not one of your good promises have failed—all have come to pass. Forgive me for the times I have not consulted with You, and forgive me for the compromises I have made to allow sin to remain in my life. I need Your strength, courage, and counsel as I reassess my work and life decisions. I am at Your mercy. Amen.

THE SEDUCTIVE POWER OF PROSPERITY

Read: Judges 2:11-23 (2-3 minutes)
And there arose another generation after them who did not know the LORD or the work that he had done for Israel.

DISCUSS + MEDITATE

After the death of Joshua, the book of Judges describes a period of Israel's history that lasts approximately 300 years until the time of the prophet Samuel. This book could just as easily be titled Deliverers as it covers twelve civil and military leaders who God raised up to deliver the people of Israel from some very difficult, self-induced situations.

The Israelites had conquered, inherited, and developed multiple cities into large cosmopolitan, urban centers. These were centers of art, literature, architecture, trade, politics, and wealth. These growing cities were also centers of Baal and Ashtaroth worship[29]. The book of Judges ultimately highlights the fact that Yahweh was the real Judge and Deliverer—He was the infallible God against the backdrop of Israel's fallibility. It's the story of the downward spiral of their national and spiritual life into chaos and apostasy, which naturally led to the emergence of a godly king and the adoption of a monarchy.

The beginning of Judges reminds us that Israel failed miserably to complete the conquest of the land. The tribe of Benjamin didn't deal with the Jebusites (1:21). Manasseh failed (1:27). Ephraim failed (1:29). Zebulun failed (1:30). And so on. This failure

to obey Yahweh would have significant consequences for generations to come. Because the people of Israel did not obey Yahweh's voice (2:2), they experienced perpetual difficulties and became ensnared by the Canaanite gods (2:3). Then the text states another issue: "There arose another generation after them who did not know the LORD or the work that he had done for Israel" (2:10). Not only that, but the people of Israel intentionally did evil by serving false gods—the Baals and the Ashtaroth (2:11-13). Baal was the pagan god of nature—specifically of storms, rain, and the land—and was symbolized with the image of a bull, taking on various additional characteristics in different geographic regions of the Fertile Crescent. The Ashtaroth (Astarte/Ishtar) was a companion goddess of fertility, love, and war. Many other goddesses of the ancient world found their origins in Astarte including Aphrodite (Greek), Venus (Roman), Athena (Greek), Diana (Roman), and Artemis (Greek).

The text states that the Israelites "served" these particular gods (2:11,13; 3:6). They saw Yahweh as a past-tense deity who delivered their people from bondage in Egypt and led them through the wilderness for forty years into the land that He had promised. But they saw no future with Him per se. And as they lived among the Canaanites,

[29]Discussed in more detail in subsequent devotionals

they also began marrying them and adding their gods into a growing pantheon of deities (3:5-6). This attempted "blending" of religions–adding other gods to the worship of Yahweh is called "syncretism." Israel considered Yahweh still relevant, but Baal and Ashtaroth were about the weather, land, and fertility—all the practical things they needed for survival and prosperity. So, if an Israelite couple wanted to get pregnant and have a healthy baby, they would reflect on Yahweh's provision of the past but include worship of the Ashtaroth in an attempt to ensure fertility.

Israel's worship of Yahweh took on more and more forms of false worship. And thus, a pattern began: apostasy—abandonment of Yahweh; servitude—punishment through slavery; supplication—crises to God for deliverance; and eventually, salvation—God's mercy in pitying Israel and raising up a deliverer to rescue them. God was and is a compassionate God—slow to anger, but abundant in grace and covenant love.

REFLECT + ACT

» We are reminded in this passage that success wasn't automatic from generation to generation. The same is true today. We can't assume that our children or students or those we employ or manage will just pick up and embrace our faith in God naturally. Making sure children experience a context that reinforces God's instructions (think—church, private school, or Bible study group), doesn't always correlate to their personal faith and obedience. We have to be intentional in working to reach the heart of the next generation and those within our sphere of influence. Morality, conservatism, and even biblical worldview

training can fall short of addressing the heart.

» Think about the religious syncretism of the Israelites, or what I call "easy-going syncretism"—blending of paganism with biblical truth. Baal and Ashtaroth might not be overtly worshiped today, but the spirit of those false gods is alive still, even in churches[30]. These false gods cultivated sensuality and promiscuity, all with a covenant-breaking spirit. They seduced with the promise of prosperity and security. Take a moment to ask God to reveal any ways you might be allowing worldly beliefs or practices into your life. Perhaps it's as simple as trying to maintain a dual existence where you worship God on Sundays but live for the world the rest of the week. Or maybe you are trying to believe God's Word while also giving deference to the universe or astrology to guide you each day. If you believe you need to add some other force or deity beyond the Creator-God into your life and work in order to be successful, then you are most likely guilty of syncretism. Take advantage of this opportunity to confess this to God and receive His grace and mercy. Turn from these idols and trust in God alone. He is abundant in covenant love.

PRAYER

Infallible God and true Deliverer of Your people, I relate with the children of Israel in this passage from the book of Judges. I'm prone to wander and go after the gods of this world. Thank you for this gracious reminder of Your steadfast love and faithfulness. Reveal any ways I have been trying to syncretize worship of You with other ideas. I am at Your mercy. Amen.

[30]Some social media groups today are still dedicated to learning about Astarte and awakening the "goddess within."

DIVINE AGENDA VS. PERSONAL AMBITION

24

Read: Judges 6:11-27 (3-4 minutes)
And they cried out, "A sword for the LORD and for Gideon!"

DISCUSS + MEDITATE

The downward spiral of Israel's national and spiritual life continues throughout Judges 3-16 as they repeated the cycle of apostasy, servitude, supplication, and salvation. But through it all, Yahweh shows He is the Chief Operator, sometimes acting silently in the background or letting His people go their own way. Chapters 3-5 of the book of Judges highlight a series of deliverers, also called judges, that God used to rescue His people from various oppressors.

Yahweh used Othniel to end eight years of oppression that then led to forty years of peace (3:7-11). He used Ehud to end eighty years of Moabite dominance in a comic-book-like assassination of an obese ruler named Eglon (3:12-30). He used Shamgar, who was actually a foreign mercenary under the service of the Egyptian pharaoh (3:31), a reminder that God can use any means to accomplish His ultimate purpose. And chapters 4 and 5 introduce the reader to Barak and the prophetess Deborah who are used by God to deliver His people after twenty years in bondage.

But the narrator of the book of Judges then spends three chapters on the life and leadership of a judge named Gideon (Judg. 6-8). Though he came from a wealthy, aristocratic family, they were the least in his particular clan, and Gideon was the least in his family. As a result, he had a complex about his capabilities.

But the LORD saw him as a mighty man of valor and promised to be with Gideon as He commissioned him to deal with the Midianites, the group of people involved in the sale of Joseph (Gen. 37) and from which Moses' wife and father-in-law Jethro originated. So, reluctantly, Gideon obeyed Yahweh and destroyed the altar of Baal that his family had sponsored at their home and the Asherah, an idol made of wood. God was using Gideon and "the Spirit of the LORD clothed" him (6:34).

But soon after, Gideon demonstrated unbelief by requesting a sign from God and trying to manipulate Him by way of a wool fleece (6:36-40). Even though Gideon was weak in faith, Yahweh, as Commander-in-Chief of Israel, miraculously empowered him and enabled Gideon and a small army of only 300 men to defeat 120,000 Midianite fighters. This success specifically glorified God's power: Yahweh had led Gideon to pare down his troop levels from

32,000 to 300, creating a scenario where Gideon could not boast in his own ability.

Sadly, Gideon continued to turn toward self-centeredness and fear and away from Yahweh as he took on campaigns that were more personal and less about defending the reputation of Yahweh. He even began attacking other Israelite tribes, dealing with them in a brutal, harsh way. In one shocking incident, he demanded his followers to hand over all of their gold jewelry so that he could make an ephod, essentially an idol like Baal that he hoped would give him insight and direction (8:22-27). Ironically, he chose to construct this new idol in the exact place where he had destroyed Baal on his family property, and he used the royal garments worn by the defeated kings of Midian to clothe his new god. The text eerily states that "all Israel whored after it there, and it became a snare to Gideon and to his family" (8:27). Instead of being an image-bearer of Yahweh who was clothed with the Holy Spirit, Gideon crafted his own useless image and clothed it with pagan materials.

This event marked the first time a leader of Israel officially sponsored an idol. Gideon's downward spiral continued, yet Yahweh remained faithful. His godless choices were vividly on display in the tragic life of his son Abimelech (chapter 9). Ultimately, Gideon leaves a sad legacy: He was a leader who was consumed with the politics of power, and he exchanged the servant leadership style of Moses for the crass, self-centered style of Canaanite rulers.

REFLECT + ACT

» Gideon's sign of the fleece is still used erroneously today as a faulty model for determining the will of God. Why is this idea problematic? First of all, the people of God are never to tempt God or try to force Him to verify His commands. Secondly, Gideon already knew God's will, but he stubbornly requested a sign to gain some sort of reassurance before actually obeying what God had said. Additionally, God was under no obligation to respond. He only graciously did so as part of accomplishing His plan of getting rid of the Midianites. So, think twice before using Gideon's methods as a model for decision-making. To require God to prove Himself is essentially trying to manipulate Him.

» God is also under no obligation to bless or lead those who bear His name in vain, who claim to be the people of God but act like Canaanites. Consider how often we are left depending on secular business principles and social sciences because we've decreased our dependence on God and slowed in our spiritual development. God's timeless Word is highly relevant for us today, helping us to know how to live and work in a way that honors Him. This is one of the primary purposes of this entire Wisdom Calling devotional series—to help you listen to God's voice as He has revealed Himself in the Word, discern what He would have for you, and cultivate the wisdom needed to live every moment strategically.

» The stories of the judges have much to teach us about leadership. It seems that the more impressive a leader's achievements, the stronger the temptation to become self-centered and independent of God, even in the context of church work and ministry. You can probably think of prominent pastors and spiritual leaders who reached a certain level of success and yet, in the end, lost it all because of failures in their private lives. Sadly, this phenomenon happens far too often. There is a constant pull for those in leadership to prioritize their own personal ambition versus God's agenda, timing, and methods. If you are currently in a leadership position or preparing to serve as a ministry leader, allow Gideon's story to sober you and provide you with greater awareness of the spiritual challenges of ministry. If you are not in a leadership role, allow this to motivate you to pray for the leaders in your life.

PRAYER

God, You are always in control, often quietly orchestrating the circumstances of my life. Would You sober me with the reminders of these fallible leaders, and would you draw me closer to You in a deeper resolve to follow Your Word? By Your Spirit and strength, would You continue to help me cultivate a heart of wisdom? Amen.

NOTES

PROFILE OF A WASTED LIFE

Read: Judges 13:1-5; 13:24-25; 16:28-30 (3-4 minutes)

And Samson said, "Let me die with the Philistines." Then he bowed with all his strength, and the house fell upon the lords and upon all the people who were in it. So the dead whom he killed at his death were more than those whom he had killed during his life.

DISCUSS + MEDITATE

As if things couldn't get any worse for Israel, they continued to be their own worst enemies. The downward spiral of their national and spiritual life sank deeper under the leadership of Samson. He followed six other judges after the death of Gideon, but he actually accomplished less than any of the others.

Israel had continued to do evil in the sight of Yahweh, and as a result He gave them into the hands of a foreign nation, the Philistines again, for forty years. But true to His character, Yahweh raised up a deliverer—Samson, a man specifically chosen, gifted, and blessed by the Spirit of God. On the surface, Samson was endowed with many abilities and opportunities, more so than any other judge that preceded him. However, the narrator paints a picture of an impressive young man who, in many ways, failed to lead his nation or follow the agenda of Yahweh.

As the story unfolds, it becomes clear that Samson, with such hope and promise, chose to rebel against his family and God's calling on his life in order to pursue his own self-centered interests. He had no regard for God's claim on his life as he married a woman outside of the nation of Israel, an act strictly forbidden by Yahweh. This act of disobedience would lead to conflict, highlighting the interplay between divine sovereignty and human motives. Samson operated all on his own, motivated by lust and power. But all along, Yahweh was in control, using even a lion as an agent of His sovereign authority.

As part of one of his vengeful escapades, Samson tied lit torches to the tails of three hundred jackals and sent them in the wheat fields at harvest time, essentially destroying the local economy (15:4-5). As Samson's enemies attempted to capture him, the text states that the Spirit of the LORD rushed upon him, enabling him to escape (15:14), but he would immediately retaliated again by using the jawbone of a donkey to kill one thousand Philistines. In the form of a victory song, Samson exclaimed how he had accomplished this feat on his own (15:15-16). Exhausted from the fight, he surprisingly cried out to Yahweh. But his prayer was only an attempt to verbalize his accomplishments and his needs—he was thirsty and needed protection from his enemy (15:18).

Chapter 16 unfolds like a spy movie—with a heroic male lead, a female agent, money, love, death, and ironic twists. Samson continued to be his own worst enemy, first as he indulged in a prostitute and then as he let himself be seduced by a Philistine woman named Delilah. He exhibited extra-human physical strength fighting men, but virtually no strength at all when it comes to women. This was due, in part, to him not taking his strength or his special calling seriously. Even toward the end of his life, when he was most likely in his forties, he flippantly relied on his own power and ingenuity. Delilah had continued to seduce him into divulging the secret of his physical strength, and ultimately, he gave in. After his enemies shaved his head while he slept, the text says Samson didn't even know that Yahweh had left him (16:20). His strength was gone.

Samson's final, climactic act occurred in the temple of Dagon[31] in front of thousands of people, including the governors of the Philistines. Samson, with eyes gouged out, cried out to Yahweh one last time. But true to character, he centered the prayer on himself— "remember me," "strengthen me," "let me get revenge," "my two eyes," "let me die." Summoning his remaining strength, Samson pushed over the main support beams, causing the temple to collapse and killing himself along with his enemies. He ironically accomplished more in his death, in terms of preserving the nation of Israel, than he did in twenty years as their deliverer.

REFLECT + ACT

» Samson in many ways mirrored the nation of Israel as a whole. Samson, like Israel, did everything possible to destroy himself, but God, Who was rich in mercy and faithful to His promises, saw to it that he wasn't ultimately successful. In fact, Yahweh's gracious intervention—something Samson seemed almost unaware of–was the only real positive feature in Samson's life. God was at work through Samson to preserve His name and His cosmic mission of grace on behalf of His people. And the same is true today. We might act like we are the masters of our own fate, but God's hidden providence is always at work behind the scenes of our lives, even when we disobey, sin, and nearly destroy ourselves. Allow this truth to bring about humility and gratitude.

» The life of Samson is one of great tragedy. He was blessed with so much from God yet squandered it away in self-centered pursuits. He didn't take his gifting seriously but rather lived by what he considered right in his own eyes. His morality consisted of doing unto others as they had done to him, a common worldly philosophy today. He had no thought of God's people or agenda. He was only concerned about using his power to try and manipulate God to get what he wanted. Samson also demonstrated little respect for women, seeing them as objects to be exploited and controlled. Sadly, his profile sounds eerily similar to many business and political leaders in our times. This is the prevailing business culture that many of us operate in each day, one driven by money, lust, and power. What an

---

[31]Dagon was the patron god of the Philistines, god of agriculture and harvest and considered to be the father of Baal.

opportunity we have as the people of God to offer something different.

PRARYER

Sovereign LORD, this is such a tragic profile of a wasted life. Thank You for including this story in Your Word, for preserving it these thousands of years. Give me eyes to see and ears to hear what You would have for me. You have set me apart to serve You and have blessed me in so many ways. I want my life and work to count. I don't want to waste my gifts. Give me the strength I need today to carry out Your mission and not my own. I'm an instrument in Your hands—to the praise of Your grace. Amen.

NOTES

MINISTRY LLC

Read: Judges 17:1-18:1 (3-4 minutes)

And he restored the 1,100 pieces of silver to his mother. And his mother said, "I dedicate the silver to the LORD from my hand for my son, to make a carved image and a metal image."

DISCUSS + MEDITATE

After a focus on the twelve judges of Israel, the narrator of the book of Judges now highlights how Israel's apostasy had trickled down to individuals within the tribes.

Chapter 17 begins with the story of a man named Micah who stole quite a bit of silver from his wealthy mother, confessed to her, and then restored it all back to her. She even blessed Yahweh as a result (17:1-2). But then she wanted him to use some of the silver to make an idol to Yahweh, so Micah made household gods, an ephod, and a shrine in their home. He even ordained one of his sons to serve as a household priest.

Micah's story shows the depth of how Canaanized Israel had become in their efforts to syncretize true worship of Yahweh with unacceptable practices of false worship. They violated God's command to have no idols (Ex.20:40-5). And they disregarded the laws about where worship should take place and about who was to serve as priests (a role reserved for those from the tribe of Levi). This is why the narrator reminds the reader, "In those days there was no king in Israel.

Everyone did what was right in his own eyes" (17:6).

A second incident involving Micah elaborates on Israel's apostasy. An actual Levite traveled through Micah's town and interacted with him. This felt like a sudden, golden opportunity: Micah recruited this Levite and made an offer the Levite couldn't refuse—to live in Micah's home and be his personal priest. Unfortunately, this Levite[32] seemed to have no sense of divine calling and no responsibilities, so he took the path of least resistance and accepted the job. This newly appointed priest-for-hire was now set with a place to live, a position, an expense account, and some fancy new outfits. And Micah thought he had followed God's rules by hiring a priest from the tribe of Levi. "Now I know the LORD will prosper me, because I have a Levite as priest," he exclaimed (17:13). For Micah, this was a chance to capitalize on a religious leader, one susceptible to money and prestige, in order to essentially manipulate God.

But chapter 18 details how quickly this opportunity for Micah changed. A group of Israelites from the tribe of Dan heard of Micah's wealth and traveled to take his

[32]Whom we later learn was named Jonathan and was the grandson of Moses

idol, household gods, and other idolatrous paraphernalia. They even lured Micah's priest away with the promise of more money and a broader exposure for his "ministry" (18:19-20). Next, the Danites decided for purely humanistic reasons to destroy the people of another town, Laish, known as quiet, wealthy, safe people (18:7). After burning Laish to the ground, these men changed the name of the city to Dan in honor of their tribe, took Jonathan the Levite for their priest, and set up Micah's idol for themselves (18:29-31).

Everyone indeed was doing what was right in their own eyes and there still remained no king in Israel.

REFLECT + ACT

» Religious syncretism, mentioned in several of these devotionals, is dangerous. In today's Bible reading, Micah and his mother appeared to try and worship Yahweh but used unacceptable and idolatrous means. They were sincere but still pagan. This version of syncretism is becoming more prevalent today: Individuals believe in God and respect Jesus but also look to Buddha or astrology for enlightenment and guidance. They might even attend a Bible-teaching church but also consult a horoscope each morning. The God of the Bible, the one true God, is a jealous God and demands that His people be exclusively devoted to Him. This may sound harsh and restrictive, especially in our increasingly tolerant society, but it's true and biblical nonetheless. It's helpful for us to remember that we cannot truly worship God while worshiping other gods or with means that are unacceptable, regardless of how sincere we might be.

» Consider reading *A Field Guide on False Teaching,* a helpful resource produced by Ligonier Ministries.[33]

» Take a minute to think about the role of pragmatism and opportunism in this passage. Micah attempted to gain favor with God by gaining favor with religious leaders. But the Levite was willing to go along and take advantage of Micah's man-made religious system. They both were pragmatists and opportunists for their own advantage. It appears Micah treated his personal, in-house religious leader like a good luck charm, a means of trying to manipulate God to bring blessing and success. And the relationship appealed to the priest's egos and ambition as well. The religious leader was driven by pragmatics, not by theological conviction. His "spiritual service" was not based on the call of God, but rather on the opportunity for personal gain.

» This same kind of arrangement can happen easily in churches today-- successful business people courting the closeness and favor of their pastors in an effort to supposedly curry more favor from God, and pastors showing partiality to the rich and wealthy in order to take advantage of the opportunity for personal gain. Success is not necessarily a sign of righteousness or an indication that we are doing something right. Sometimes it is the opposite. May God grant us the discernment we need to examine our own hearts and motives and behave wisely and biblically.

[33]https://www.ligonier.org/store/a-field-guide-on-false-teaching-paperback

PRAYER

God, would You help me examine my heart to check my motives? I want to first of all worship You alone, and I want to do so by means that honor You. I also want to avoid getting close to spiritual leaders as some sort of way of gaining favor with You. I want my motives to be pure and want the spiritual leaders in my life to serve in ways that are free from ego, pragmatism, and the quest for prestige. We are at Your mercy. Amen.

NOTES

GOD'S REAL ESTATE

27

Read: Ruth 4:1-12 (3-4 minutes)

Then the women said to Naomi, "Blessed be the LORD, who has not left you this day without a redeemer, and may his name be renowned in Israel!"

DISCUSS + MEDITATE

The book of Ruth, set "in the days when the judges ruled" (1:1), comes as a breath of fresh air after the dark and depressing days of the judges that we've just considered over the past four devotionals. It's a story of how God's people experience His wisdom, sovereignty, and covenant kindness, often disguised in difficult circumstances and mediated through the actions of others.

Ruth records how a famine in Judah forced a woman named Naomi, her husband Elimelech, and their two sons to leave Israel and move to Moab. While there, the two sons married Moabite women. One of those women was named Ruth. After about ten years, Naomi's husband and sons died, leaving the remaining women destitute. Naomi returned back to her original home in Bethlehem after the famine, and her daughter-in-law Ruth chose to go with her. Ruth providentially met and married a relative of Naomi named Boaz, and the descendants of this family eventually included King David and even Jesus the Messiah.

The famine, the move to Moab, and then the untimely death of Naomi's husband and sons left Naomi economically bankrupt and socially vulnerable. Her present was without men and provision, and her future was without hope. But upon hearing that "Yahweh had visited his people and given them food," she was determined to return to her homeland (1:6). Naomi then offered a prayer for Yahweh, asking Him to "deal kindly" with them (the Hebrew word is *hesed*) and grant them rest to her family (1:8). This Hebrew concept of *hesed*, often translated into English as "kindness," combines multiple qualities of Yahweh into one character trait. It's a word that describes God's faithful love and loyalty to the covenant He has made with His people. *Hesed* encompasses love, mercy, grace, goodness, benevolence, loyalty, and covenant faithfulness. It's a love focused more on action than on emotion, and it is always aimed at benefiting the person loved.

As a non-Israelite, Ruth demonstrates incredible, unexpected commitment to Naomi and unexpected submission to the God of Israel by insisting on returning to Israel with Naomi (1:16-17). It is a blessing to see how the hidden hand of God continued to lead these women as they settled into Bethlehem and Ruth began to work in the wheat and barley fields owned by Boaz, an upstanding man and one of Naomi's relatives. With a tone of grace and generosity, Boaz advised her to stick close to his other workers and then asked God to bless and care for her as a mother bird protects her chicks (2:8-13).

Chapter 3 highlights an approach used by Naomi and Ruth to get Boaz's attention. The circumstances were used by God to lead Boaz to marry Ruth and to buy the land formerly owned by Naomi's deceased husband. Boaz recognized Yahweh's *hesed* to him through Ruth, and in the end he decided to redeem Naomi's land in a public negotiation and contract deliberation at the city gates. Ultimately, this is just the backstory of how Yahweh would preserve the family line of David, the eventual monarch of Israel—a story of Yahweh's fierce commitment to His promises and people.

REFLECT + ACT

» This short book of Ruth primarily reminds us of the kind, and often quiet, providence of God—His sovereign control over and involvement in every single thing. He was in control of nature in withholding rains in Israel, which led to a famine and forced people like Naomi to relocate. God was in control over seeming chance events, like when Ruth just "happened" to come to the part of the land owned by Boaz (2:3). But this wasn't the pagan concept of fate or the popular ideas of "luck" or "fortune." This was the actual orchestration of events and circumstances by God's guiding hand. God's providence was even at work in plans organized by Ruth and Naomi for Ruth's marriage. And we see His providence on

display through the legal process and real estate negotiations. And guess what? This same God is still in control and at work in the mundane circumstances of our lives today. Believe it, my friend. Allow the story of Ruth to encourage you in your faith in God. He is kind. He is gracious. And He never changes! In our current culture that changes very rapidly from day to day and from quarter to quarter, we are loved by God and in a covenantal relationship with the One Who will always exist and will always be the same. He is worthy of our trust and commitment.

» Ruth further teaches us modern readers that we are able to demonstrate love and benevolence to others because God has consistently demonstrated His loving loyalty to us. True covenant love (*hesed*) is expressed by concern for the welfare of others, demonstrated through ethical character and actions. Ruth demonstrated this kind of love to Naomi, and Boaz demonstrated this to Ruth and his workers. Boaz's *hesed* was evident in the kind of work environment he created, his blessing of his employees, the graciousness of his speech, and his choice to eat with them (2:4-6; 14). He even instituted the first biblically recorded anti-sexual harassment policy in the workplace (2:8-9). This kind of love is desperately needed in the business world today, a world where ruthless and cutthroat behavior toward competitors and even clients is rewarded. The corporate world today applauds those who take advantage of people. What an opportunity you and I have to offer a completely different way of doing business—one that employs wisdom and shrewdness and celebrates kindness and graciousness.

» Listen to the song "Promises" by Maverick City Music (2020).

PRAYER

Yahweh, is there anyone more loving and faithful than You? I praise You right now in response to the story of Naomi and Ruth and Boaz, thanking You for Your providential hand at work in the circumstances of their lives and times. Great is Your faithfulness! Thank You for loving me even in the midst of my unfaithfulness to You. Help me today to reflect this love in and through my work. I want to be known not only for my success, but more importantly for the kindness and graciousness I demonstrate to others. Amen.

INTERLUDE

The last few devotionals have covered approximately three hundred years of Israel's history. These events took place between Joshua's departure at the end of the patriarch period, through the days of the judges, and continuing up to the time of Samuel and the monarchy. After Joshua, the people of Israel continued their spiritual decline, turning away from God's Word and doing what was right in their own eyes. The pattern continued: they sinned against God; He disciplined them by sending them into captivity under a neighboring people; they cried out to God; and He was merciful and sent a deliverer.

Ultimately, each of these deliverers or judges failed to fully protect and provide for the people, and most failed at faithfully representing Yahweh. Instead of simply following Yahweh, the people grew in their desire for a human king, one they thought would finally protect and provide for them in a way they thought they deserved.

These next devotionals are rooted in this new period of transition away from a *theocracy* (rule by God) to a *monarchy* (rule by one person). The people of Israel certainly needed a king, but the perfect King would not be realized until the Messiah came. The line of offspring leading to the Messiah (Christ) continued through the tribe of Judah to Boaz to David. Boaz, as Ruth's kinsman-redeemer, prefigured Christ for His people, as would some of the future kings, especially David.

The devotionals studying books of 1 and 2 Samuel will be intertwined with some focused on relevant Psalms written during this same period of Israel's history. These psalms serve not only as an additional source of historical information but also as a divine commentary on human life and the wisdom you and I can gain from reading it.

Samuel is the link between judgeship and kingship. In our study, we will see God exercising His cosmic kingship by inaugurating a dynasty in Israel, starting with a man named David, and electing the city of Jerusalem as the place where David's successor would establish the temple for the worship of the divine king Yahweh. David is at the center of God's plan of salvation and still subject to His Word, will, and providential guidance. May this same God grant to you a fresh understanding of His faithfulness as you continue through these next devotionals.

NOTES

OVERWHELMING ANXIETY + INFINITE GOD

Read: 1 Samuel 1:1-2; 1:19-20; 1:27-28; 2:11; 2:26; 3:1; 3:19; 7:3-4; 7:12 (3-4 minutes)
And Samuel said to all the house of Israel, "If you are returning to the LORD with all your heart, then put away the foreign gods and the Ashtaroth from among you and direct your heart to the LORD and serve him only, and he will deliver you . . ."

DISCUSS + MEDITATE

The book of 1 Samuel begins with a distressed woman named Hannah (whose name meant "grace"), a woman who in God's providence would become the mother of the king-maker. The text tells us that she had not been able to have children and to make things worse, the other wife of her husband constantly harassed her. Her rival emotionally and psychologically afflicted her in such a way that she wouldn't eat, wept continuously, and was troubled in her spirit (1:6-16). This led to severe anxiety. But in the midst of this horrible situation, Hannah was bold enough to believe that God would hear and answer her prayer for a son. She prayed to "Yahweh of hosts," a title for the Lord which referenced the armies of God and their infinite resources and power (1:11). And Yahweh heard her cry and provided her a son whom she called Samuel, a name that means "heard of God."

The second chapter of 1 Samuel records Hannah's prayer (2:1-10), which reflects her confident trust in the God Who controls and judges the whole world. She no longer had to be controlled by anxiety. Instead, she could live with an unshakeable assurance in Yahweh the Rock (v. 2). He is the One Who has no place for the proud and arrogant (v. 3). He's the One Who can change a person's status in life in an instant (vv. 7-8). He is the One Who has set the social and moral order of society (v. 8) and Who ultimately would anoint His "anointed" (Messiah) (v. 10). The text says that Samuel "grew in the presence of Yahweh" (2:21) and that he "continued to grow both in stature and in favor with Yahweh and man" (2:26). He stood in contrast to the wicked, self-serving priests he apprenticed under. We are reminded of the current state of our world as we read of Samuel's culture: "The word of Yahweh was rare in those days; there was no frequent vision" (3:1). Samuel would soon be used to change that reality as he was called by God to be His mouthpiece (3:2-20).

Israel soon suffered a defeat by the Philistines, who captured the ark of the covenant for seven months. The people of Israel naively thought that just the presence of the ark would ensure their deliverance, but Yahweh had removed His presence: "The glory has departed" (4:21). The Philistines took the ark as a trophy and

---

placed it in their temple to Dagon[34]. But Yahweh intervened by causing the statue of Dagon to topple over and by inflicting the Philistines with tumors: "The hand of Yahweh was heavy against [them]" (5:9).

These enemies of God eventually sent the ark back, thus signifying the start of the repentance process for the people of Israel (chapter 6). In a defining moment, Samuel summoned the entire nation together and exhorted them to turn back to Yahweh "with all [their] heart," to turn away from their false gods of fertility and harvest, and to "direct [their] heart to the Lord and serve him only" (7:3). And miraculously, the people did repent and served Yahweh with a singular focus (7:4). This would set the stage for the new monarchy.

REFLECT + ACT

» Hannah's situation reminds us of the reality of anxiety and emotional trauma. In her case, it was triggered by her barrenness and the constant harassment of her rival. So often in the business community, we are encouraged to just "suck it up" or "deal with it" when we experience trials on the job or in our personal lives. Thankfully, in recent years there has been a much-needed increase in mental health resources, concern for social-emotional wellbeing, and work-life balance initiatives. While we applaud these advances in corporate culture, we need to be discerning about the self-centered and godless nature of many such remedies. Our true emotional wellbeing isn't the sum benefit of self-care and wise stress management, but rather an intentional, sustained resting in the LORD of hosts, the

One Who has infinite power and resources to meet our every need, even the ones most deep within our souls. As a former professor of mine used to say, "It's not the *amount* of our faith that matters—it's the *object* of our faith." Social-emotional well being measures and prayer aren't mutually exclusive. The problem comes when we merely rely on those measures, techniques, and strategies and fail to trust in the Lord. Take this opportunity to turn from any self-reliant means you have been employing to minimize your anxiety. Place your faith in Him.

» I want to highlight in a bit more detail the presence of God in Samuel's life. Consider these verses once again: "Samuel grew in the presence of the LORD" (2:21); "Samuel continued to grow both in stature and in favor with the LORD and also with man" (2:26); "And Samuel grew, and the LORD was with him and let none of his words fall to the ground" (3:19); "for he said, 'Till now the LORD has helped us'" (7:12). Samuel grew and developed and was ultimately used greatly because God's hand was on his life. So, here's my question: *Is God's hand upon your life?* I don't ask this to trouble you in any way or cause doubt. But I want to exhort you either to be encouraged by the clear evidence of His presence in your life or to consider why it seems like His presence isn't currently with you. If you are concerned about the latter, I encourage you to take this a step further and start the process of interacting with a trusted, biblical advisor. You can have all the success in the world, but without God, in the end it will be written over your life and work, "The glory has departed."

PRAYER

Yahweh of hosts, You alone have infinite resources and power. My anxiety at times seems to be infinite because I've allowed my problems to become so big and Your presence so small. Forgive me. I want to turn to You once again and away from the constant presence of false gods all around me. Speak, LORD! I want to hear Your voice and have the strength and courage to obey. As Your child, remind me of Your faithful presence today. Amen.

NOTES

THE KING-MAKER

29

Read: 1 Samuel 12:13-25 (3-4 minutes)

"Has not the LORD anointed you to be prince over his people Israel? And you shall reign over the people of the LORD and you will save them from the hand of their surrounding enemies."

DISCUSS + MEDITATE

At the start of chapter eight of 1 Samuel, the prophet Samuel is now an old man. To delegate his leadership, he set his sons up as judges, but the text states that these young men did not follow their father Samuel's ways but instead went after gain, took bribes, and perverted justice (8:1-3). To make matters worse, the elders and people of Israel kept demanding a king to rule over them. They wanted to be like all the other nations. They wanted influence, status, and ultimately someone with the responsibility to protect them in addition to Yahweh (8:4-9; 19-22).

This desire never set well with Samuel, and he repeatedly rebuked the people for this clear effort to turn from dependence on Yahweh. He even tried to paint a realistic picture of what life under a king would be like for them—the pros and cons. A king would need their sons to drive his chariots, to command his troops, to work his fields, and to make weapons. A king would need their daughters to make perfume, cook, and bake. Israel would be required to give up a portion of their vineyards and orchards and would have to pay a tax of a tenth of their grain and flocks (8:10-18).

The story of chapter nine tells us that Israel did not listen to Samuel's counsel. It begins with a very wealthy man named Kish who had a tall and handsome son named Saul (9:1-2). Kish sent his son out to go find some donkeys, but the episode highlights the providence of God in orchestrating the circumstances of man—in this case, a man who would be His anointed one over His people.

Yahweh revealed to Samuel that Saul was in fact His divinely appointed leader for the new monarchy. Samuel and Saul then had what might appear to be a chance run-in, but it was truly ordered by God: Samuel told Saul that he was chosen by God to be king. At this point, we start to learn that Saul has many emotional ups and downs as he moves into his role as a king. When Samuel disclosed God's selection of Saul as king, Saul instantly wanted nothing to do with this job. But Samuel went on to coronate him as king in a private ceremony (10:1-8). And as Saul left, the text states that God "gave him another heart" (10:9). Then, leading up to the public proclamation of Saul as king, he was found hiding. And while most of the people were thrilled, shouting "Long live the king!" others had no faith in Saul (10:24-27). But the Spirit of God empowered Saul, and his first major victory came in the form of defeating the Ammonites, thus uniting the kingdom. At this point, Saul was still in right relation with God as he proclaimed, "Yahweh has worked salvation in Israel" (11:1-15).

Samuel took this occasion to address the people of Israel and remind them of his leadership over two generations and the sovereignty of God from the beginning. Samuel had "made a king" for them, even against his personal beliefs about the wisdom of a monarchy (12:1). He lived and led them with integrity, never stealing or accepting bribes (12:2-5).

But then, Samuel cataloged for Israel all the ways Yahweh had provided for them—from the time of their exodus from Egypt, through their Sinai wanderings, and into Canaan (12:6-13). He reminded the people that if they feared Yahweh appropriately and feared the king also, then it would be well with them (12:14-15). Samuel exhorted them to not be afraid, but to serve Yahweh with all their hearts, and to turn from "empty things" that would keep them from serving the Lord (12:20-21).

Ultimately, both the new king and the people existed for Yahweh's glory, His pleasure, and for His fame among all the nations (12:22). But Israel needed to fear God and serve Him and use that time of transition to look back and "consider what great things [God had] done" (12:24). If they remained faithful in this, all would be well with the kingdom. Only time would tell whether Saul would lead in this way.

REFLECT + ACT

» God sometimes, perhaps even often, allows us to go our own way–as He allowed Israel to experience a monarchy. And when this happens, it doesn't mean God has relinquished any of His control in our lives, but He does put us in situations where we are vulnerable and open to negative consequences. Make it a habit to try and think through decisions from a 360-degree view, including the primary work of considering God's will in the situation, and also the process of doing a cost-benefit analysis to weigh the pros and cons of the decision. Bringing wise believers into the process is an additional great approach. Those not immediately connected to the situation can often provide an unbiased perspective.

» The people of Israel were motivated to have a king because they wanted to be like the other nations: they craved influence and status. This was a focus on the here-and-now, the temporal. When we compare ourselves with others or seek to impress people, whether in person or through social media, this can often lead to poor decisions—spending money on things to show off or give the appearance of success, over-emphasis on our physical appearance, high-octane competitiveness just to win at all costs, etc. What is your motivation in life and at work? Is your aim aligned with the goals of God's glory and the good of others? Are you focused on unhealthy comparison of yourself to others?

» We live in a culture of excessive individualism where we let our rights, identities, dreams, desires, and personal brands become the center of our universe.

Yet, we are reminded in this section of Scripture that we exist for God's name, for His reputation and fame. It pleases Him when we defer our rights and root our identities in Him, when we dream within His will and have desires that align with His Word and mission.

» Samuel used the transition into a monarchy to call God's people to reflect on all the ways God had provided for them. Let's take this same opportunity now. Spend a few moments thinking back as far as you can in your life and even in your family history, specifically calling to remembrance people and events and places where God worked. Maybe even play the song "Goodness of God"[35] and allow your heart and mind to fill up with gratitude for His faithfulness.

PRAYER

I love You, Lord, for Your mercy never fails me. All my days, I've been held in Your hands. From the moment that I wake up, until I lay my head, oh, I will sing of the goodness of God. And all my life You have been faithful, and all my life You have been so, so good. With every breath that I am able, oh, I will sing of the goodness of God. Amen.

NOTES

OBEDIENCE > RITUAL

30

Read: 1 Samuel 15:9-31 (3-4 minutes)
And Samuel said, "Has the LORD as great delight in burnt offerings and sacrifices, as in obeying the voice of the LORD? Behold, to obey is better than sacrifice, and to listen than the fat of rams.

DISCUSS + MEDITATE

1 Samuel 13 through 15 covers the reign of Saul—a period of history marked by fights with Israel's enemies, moments of trust in God, and key times when poor decisions were made. This section begins with the newly crowned king organizing a standing army of three thousand men, as the people trembled with fear at the Philistines. The prophet Samuel was away for more than seven days, and since Samuel wasn't around to ask for Yahweh's blessing, impatient Saul decided to offer a burnt offering himself.

This action was an effort on Saul's part to "force" the situation with Yahweh (13:12), but from Samuel's perspective, Saul had acted "foolishly" in not obeying the LORD (13:13). As a result, his kingship would not continue much longer.[36] Saul's son Jonathan, armed with fervent and focused faith in Yahweh and only his armor bearer by his side, miraculously defeated a group of twenty Philistine soldiers. Jonathan believed that "the Lord will work for us" and that "nothing can hinder the Lord from saving by many or by few" (14:6). Jonathan even predicted that "Yahweh has given them into our hand" (14:12). Yahweh did intervene and caused an earthquake and great panic among the Philistines. Ultimately, "Yahweh saved Israel that day" (14:23).

But the broader Philistine threat remained. And King Saul, in an effort to ensure maximum focus amongst his soldiers, issued a rash ban for them not to eat any food for a day. Then he added on a vow that anyone who defied this order would be killed. Sadly, Jonathan had not been around to hear his father's decree, and as Jonathan's group of soldiers traveled, he came across some honeycomb and ate some of the honey (14:27). Word quickly spread back to King Saul. In the end, Jonathan publicly criticized his father for his decision that "troubled the land," almost causing many of them to die (14:29). The people sided with the beloved Jonathan and pressured the king to change his mind (14:45).

After this episode, Yahweh commanded Saul to defeat the Amalekites, a group of people who had harassed the people of Israel generations before during their wilderness wandering. Saul organized the battle and was successful, but following their victory, Saul and the people did not fully obey God. They spared the

---

[36]For an interesting case study on a commodity monopoly, read 1 Samuel 13:19-22 where the Philistines, in the Iron Age, used that innovation to their advantage.

Amalekite leader Agag, and they kept the best animals and valuable items for themselves—even though God had commanded that *all* of Amalek be devoted to destruction (15:9).

This was such an egregious choice and one that showed very poor judgment on Saul's part. As a result, Yahweh told Samuel that He had regret or sorrow that He had made Saul king (15:10, 35). But Samuel felt like this moral failure was his responsibility. He was very angry, cried all night over the situation, and was grieved over Saul's decision (15:11, 25). Saul shifted responsibility and blamed the people for the decision, but Samuel reminded Saul and Israel that Yahweh is more pleased when His people simply obey Him and not when they participate in outward religious rituals such as burnt offerings (15:22-23). Disobedience to the clear commands of God is equivalent to rebellion and idolatry—offenses He doesn't take lightly.

Saul eventually admitted a basic level of sin—giving in to the wishes of the people because of fear—but he quickly sought to maintain favor with Yahweh by asking that he retain his honor before the elders and people. He was more concerned with his image and reputation in the end, rather than the reputation of Yahweh.

King Saul did have a loyal following. He was a valiant warrior and on the surface made some attempts to acknowledge Yahweh during his reign. But full devotion of the heart to God was severely missing in this king's life. As a result, Saul later lost his kingship, setting the stage for a younger and more godly man to become Israel's second king.

REFLECT + ACT

» We can gain wisdom by taking time to analyze Saul's decision-making. He should have been advancing his army while seeking the Lord. Instead, he sat around and waited for a week, and in the end he took things into his own hands with his unlawful sacrifice. When he made a rash decision for his soldiers not to eat any food for a day, he failed to consider the immediate and long-term ramifications. It is easy to criticize Saul's choices, but the key here is for us to learn from God's Word. Sometimes it is best to move forward with action, trusting the Lord to lead, while other times it's best to take our time and solicit advice from others. The pressure is greater if you're a leader and your decisions have real-life implications. Ask God to help you grow in your discernment and in your ability to make the right decisions, in the right way, and at the right time.

» We can also develop wisdom by reflecting on Samuel's words about obedience, external rituals, and repentance. It appears that Saul exhibited a partial faith in God and a partial repentance regarding his sin and poor leadership. But he was very interested in making things appear as if nothing had happened while trying to save face before the other leaders and the people. This is a natural impulse isn't it? It's much easier to say, "Okay, maybe I could've done better," or "We all make mistakes," or "I'll try to do better next time." Instead, when we are made aware of our sin, we should call it what it is to God and ask forgiveness of those impacted by it. God is more pleased when we obey Him. To be clear, outward acts of service to Him can certainly reflect a heart of worship for Him. But outward religious ceremony (church attendance, singing, praying, giving) do not impress God–especially if we are living lives of disobedience to His Word.

>>   Listen to Travis Greene's song "Perform" and allow God to fill you with truth, rid you of shame, and relieve you of the pressure to constantly try and perform for Him and others.

PRAYER

Instead of providing a representative prayer, I'd like to encourage you to take whatever time you need to reflect, to cry out to God, to bow down in worship, etc. May our gracious heavenly Father draw us close to Him as a result of His perfect and timely Word.

NOTES

NOTES

NOTES

NOTES

TOPIC LIST
NUMBERS INDICATE WHICH DEVOTIONAL

WISDOM KEEPS CALLING

ENJOY OTHER VOLUMES OF DEVOTIONALS AS YOU
CONTINUE YOUR SEARCH.

GO TO WISDOMCALLING.ORG FOR THE LATEST, AND
SUBSCRIBE TO OUR NEWSLETTER FOR UPDATES ON NEW
BOOKS, PODCASTS, AND COURSES.

THE WISDOM CALLING PODCAST
AVAILABLE ON ALL LISTENING PLATFORMS

APPLE,
SPOTIFY,
AUDIBLE,
AMAZON MUSIC

WANT INSPIRATION, STORIES, PODCAST UPDATES, AND WAYS TO GO DEEPER?

SUBSCRIBE FOR FREE TO THE WISDOM CALLING NEWSLETTER.

www.wisdomcalling.org

ACKNOWLEDGEMENTS

Noone is truly self-made; everyone has benefited from various people, institutions, and organizations along the way. The same is true with planning, writing, editing, and formatting of any book. I have been the recipient of much insight and grace from so many over the past couple of years during the early stages of this particular project and this is my attempt to acknowledge them.

I first would like to thank my friend and former life sherpa, Dwight Gibson. As Chief Explorer of The Exploration Group, God has used the many sessions we shared together to help bring clarity and direction for me in terms of calling, vision, and vocation.

I would also like to thank Brannon McAllister for his early branding work for Wisdom Calling and Michelle Getz for the current version. She also gets credit for the design and layout of the book. Another crucial part of my team has been Abby Huffstutler, the primary editor of the devotionals. Thank you for your attention to detail and your insight.

Very early on I piloted the first five devotionals with a group of about 25 professionals around the country. Their feedback was invaluable and instrumental in the direction of this book. I want to list them here, in no particular order: Andy Henderson, Dr. Champ Thornton, Charles Hopkins, Chris Jones, Jeremy Pearson, Josh Crockett, Melissa Carlisle, Tim Joiner, Lisa McKibbon, Jaime Ostergard, Timothy Bolognone, David Shaffer and Patrick Reilly. I want to especially thank my good friend Jonathan Stanley who introduced me to the "Wedgewood Posse," a group of earnest seekers who all live in the same neighborhood. Thank you for allowing me to pilot the first ten devotionals with you gentlemen.

Ted Stricklin and Dr. Kevin Oberlin have gone above and beyond to share feedback and influence the direction of these devotionals. And finally, I want to thank Jordan Raynor for your excellent example, your encouragement, and the framework you've provided ahead of me.

Soli Deo Gloria

WISDOM CALLING: FOR LEADERS, TEAMS, AND ORGANIZATIONS

Could you, or those you lead, benefit from a Biblical wisdom perspective rooted in practical experience?

Would you like to see the culture of your organization be more effective and more *human*?

In addition to his own enterprises, Bobo Beck has been helping leaders and organizations connect their faith and work to better steward opportunities and live intentionally.

- Navigating change
- Confidence in Decisions
- Clarity in calling and career
- Growth and innovation strategies
- Delegation and healthy leadership
- Integrating faith in the marketplace
- Strategic planning
- Organizational culture

Contact Bobo at **WisdomCalling.org**

SMALL GROUP FACILITATION GUIDE

One of the most effective ways to get the most out of the daily devotionals, is to go through them alongside a small group of peers, colleagues, or those you lead.

For these 30 devotionals, consider meeting over the course of six weeks to eighteen weeks (reviewing one to five devotionals each week). Each session could last 30-90 minutes. Whatever the setting, whether in person or online, the following proven tips can help everyone have a rewarding engagement.

THE FACILITATOR'S ROLE – You don't have to be an expert or even the most experienced person in the group. But you do need to know some basics of group dynamics and facilitation. Think of your role as an air traffic controller versus a pilot; in one you are directing multiple components while in the other you are the only one flying it.

GROUP CULTURE – It will be your responsibility to set the tone for the group.. Recognize that your fellow group members have valuable insights, experiences, and perspectives. Ensure that everyone is welcome and find ways to get everyone involved as much as possible. Consider using simple ice-breakers to help members bond and get to know each other. These can include basic discussion of career path–or faith journey depending on how well you know each other.

PREPARATION – Be prepared before each meeting by clearly communicating the time, location, agenda, etc. Take some time to come up with thoughtful, open-ended questions designed to draw out great responses and discussion. This won't happen by accident; it takes intentional planning. Be sure everyone has a copy of the book well before the first meeting.

DISCUSSION – Use the majority of the time to briefly review the devotional(s) from that week. See if there are any questions about the Bible passages and clarify anything that might still be confusing. Take some time to have members share any new thoughts or perspectives that came from the devotionals. Ask participants where they might need specific answers, change, or accountability to move forward.

FOLLOW THROUGH – Be prepared to table certain discussions or questions if no clear answer is apparent. Commit to researching further throughout the week and share insights with the group perhaps in a complementary discussion forum such as a private social media group or Slack. Find ways to nurture the group throughout the week.

Remember, this is all about "The Offer of Wisdom for the Business of Living"–the goal is for wisdom to be applied practically in daily life and business decisions.

AUTHOR BIO

Bobo Beck is a maverick leader who has spent his career helping individuals and organizations in the fields of business, education, and international development.

He is the founder of Ninety Twelve Group, where he helps other leaders and entrepreneurs plan, launch, and grow their organizations through consulting and strategic planning. Through this work, he has helped to found The Judson School, a community-based private school serving the Judson Mill community in Greenville, SC.

Bobo is also the co-founder of SorenBeck Properties, a real estate investing company based in Philadelphia, Pennsylvania. He is the founder and team leader of Bobo Beck & Co., an award- winning real estate company within Berkshire Hathaway HomeServices (BHHS), one of the largest real estate brokerages in the country. In 2019, 2020, and 2021, Bobo earned the *BHHS Chairman's Circle Award,* an achievement reserved for the top 1% of agents nationwide.

He has served as the founder and executive director of a Philadelphia-based nonprofit called Urban Imperative, which, from 2004 to 2008, made it their mission to recruit and train young adults for urban ministry. In 2011, he also founded Grace Seed, a grassroots international development organization that helps incubate and support small businesses and schools in countries like Uganda, Zambia, and the Dominican Republic. To date, he has traveled to over 40 countries around the world.

Through Wisdom Calling, Bobo speaks, creates courses, consults, and coaches leaders and the organizations they serve in areas such as:
- Navigating change
- Confidence in Decisions
- Clarity in calling and career
- Growth and innovation strategies
- Delegation and healthy leadership
- Integrating faith in the marketplace
- Strategic planning
- Organizational culture

Bobo holds a bachelor and master of arts degree in Bible, a master's of education in multicultural education, and a doctorate of education in educational leadership. He has also completed multiple professional development courses from three Ivy League institutions. He currently resides in Greenville, South Carolina.

Made in the USA
Columbia, SC
08 January 2023

74889815R00057